PRAISE FOR

"*Social Equations* will quickly become a critical read for STEM leaders. Having been through many years of technical training and education, leaders and team members in STEM fields often feel unprepared for the soft skills that corporate settings require. Well-researched and expertly written, this book is the ultimate tool kit for improving your relationships and collaboration!"

—**DR. MARSHALL GOLDSMITH,** *Thinkers50* #1 Executive Coach and *New York Times* best-selling author of *The Earned Life*, *Triggers*, and *What Got You Here Won't Get You There*

"Crystal Kadakia and Janette Williams have created a timely, practical, and masterful resource to navigate social dynamics in the workplace. This extraordinarily useful book is a must-read for STEM professionals who want to grow their leadership skills to the next level. Packed with practical tools and relatable examples, this is a resource you will refer to often as you work."

—**DARLENE CHRISTOPHER,** Senior Knowledge & Learning Officer, World Bank Group

"Network intelligence, relationship management, and navigating team dynamics are modern day skills that even the most technically proficient experts need to sustain lasting, impactful careers. This modular self-paced guidebook helps you curate the most critical attributes you need in the moment, wherever you are in your professional journey. So grab a notebook and your favorite pen and get down to work with arguably the most important client of your career: yourself."

—**AUSTIN LIN,** former President & Chair of the Board of Directors, American Society for Quality

"In *Social Equations*, Kadakia and Williams provide clear framing for social capability building that should resonate with technical professionals of all levels. This book fills the gaps for successful STEM professionals who aspire to be effective leaders yet perceive that resources in this area rarely have their unique experiences in mind."

—**RAY KUNG,** Senior Manager of Tech Enablement, Reddit

"This book's innovation is to bring a practical toolbox for powerful leadership and brilliant teams directly to STEM professionals, who have so often been passed by in conversations like this. It's no exaggeration to say that STEM leaders are critical to saving the world, and *Social Equations* helps make that easier with carefully selected concepts and frameworks from psychology, behavioral econ, organizational design, and more, put into a STEM context. Single sections can stand alone to help solve immediate problems, but Kadakia and Williams also build the terms of the equations over the course of the book—zooming out from individuals to the complicated, important organizations so many STEM leaders are building."

—**PATRICK MURPHY,** ESG Consultant at Point B, member of the Sierra Club Board of Directors, and former VP of a data analytics team in fintech

"I am grateful you all have done this work because consciously navigating social dynamics is a critical piece to any project's success."

—**DR. MARGARET WHEATLEY,** author of many books including *Leadership and the New Science* and *Who Do We Choose to Be?*

**THE STEM PROFESSIONAL'S USER GUIDE
TO BUILDING POSITIVE RELATIONSHIPS**

SOCIAL EQUATIONS

**CRYSTAL KADAKIA &
JANETTE WILLIAMS**

ILLUSTRATED BY MICHELLE SMILEY

RIVER GROVE
BOOKS

Published by River Grove Books
Austin, TX
www.rivergrovebooks.com

Copyright © 2022 Crystal Kadakia, Janette S. Williams

All rights reserved.

Thank you for purchasing an authorized edition of this book and for complying with copyright law. No part of this book may be reproduced, stored in a retrieval system, or transmitted by any means, electronic, mechanical, photocopying, recording, or otherwise, without written permission from the copyright holder.

Distributed by River Grove Books

Design and composition by Greenleaf Book Group
Cover design by Greenleaf Book Group
Illustrations by Michelle Smiley

Publisher's Cataloging-in-Publication data is available.

Print ISBN: 978-1-63299-622-0

eBook ISBN: 978-1-63299-623-7

First Edition

To all my dear friends of the Upsilon Prime class of Pepperdine's MSOD program, my husband, Jeremy, and my best friend, Aaron, thank you for patiently helping me in my own journey of self-awareness and growth.

—CRYSTAL

To my husband, Butch, friends, colleagues, and students, I'm forever grateful for helping me continue to evolve into the best version of myself.

—JANETTE

To John, who has always embraced my request of "I need to see it in drawing" regardless of the application.

—MICHELLE

CONTENTS

PREFACE *ix*

PART 1:
THE FIRST
PRINCIPLE IS YOU

$N = x$

1.1 Growing Your Self-Awareness | The Johari Window *5*

1.2 Managing Your Reactions | The Four Fatal Fears *16*

1.3 Pausing and Creating Space | Mindfulness *26*

1.4 Thinking Beyond Problems, Negativity, and Deficiencies | Appreciative Inquiry *35*

1.5 Making Decisions and Taking Action | Heuristics and Perspective-Taking *46*

PART 2:
THE FIRST PRINCIPLES
OF RELATIONSHIPS

$N = x_1 + x_2$

2.1 Acting with the Nature of Relationships in Mind | The Co-Creation View *61*

2.2 Pausing When Triggered | The Ladder of Inference *73*

2.3 Inviting People In | A "Towards You" State *83*

2.4 Growing Long-Term Bonds | Givers, Matchers, and Takers *94*

PART 3:
THE FIRST PRINCIPLES OF TEAM MEMBERSHIP

$$N = \sum_{i-n}^{n} x_i$$

3.1 Expecting Realistic Performance | Team Development Lifecycle *109*

3.2 Building Team Trust | Covey's Speed of Trust Model *122*

3.3 Bringing Yourself | Psychological Safety *135*

3.4 Navigating Conflict | Crucial Conversations Model *145*

3.5 Leveraging Diversity | Polarity Thinking *156*

PART 4:
THE FIRST PRINCIPLES OF LEADING TEAMS

$$N = \frac{x_1}{\sum_{i-n}^{n} x_i}$$

4.1 Leading vs. Doing | Adaptive vs. Toxic Leadership *169*

4.2 Starting Up a Team Effort | Designing the Kickoff and Other Meetings *181*

4.3 Effectively Using Authority | Collaborative Power *194*

4.4 Making Decisions Together | Sensemaking and Decision-Making Methods *203*

4.5 Celebrating Teamwork | Closings, Feedforward, and Retrospectives *217*

PART 5:
THE FIRST PRINCIPLES OF LEADING TEAMS OF TEAMS

$$N = \frac{X_1}{\sum_{i-n}^{n} x_i + \sum_{i-n}^{n} y_i}$$

5.1 Making Sense of the Organization | Open and Complex System Theories *231*

5.2 Working with the Culture | The Beach and STAR Models *244*

5.3 Motivating and Engaging People | Intrinsic and Extrinsic Rewards *254*

5.4 Navigating Internal Politics | Defensive Routines and Collaborative Advantage *263*

5.5 Cultivating Collective Wisdom | Learning Organizations and Learner 4.0 Capability *275*

ACKNOWLEGMENTS *287*

NOTES *289*

ABOUT THE AUTHORS *297*

ABOUT THE ILLUSTRATOR *299*

PREFACE

Why did you choose a career in the science, technology, engineering, or math (STEM) field? The most common answer: to make a difference. And yet, even if you are great at the technical aspects of your job, you can still fail to have the impact you want. That's because there's a disconnect between what we are good at and what we need to be good at in order to achieve our goals. This disconnect centers on an indisputable fact of the workplace: Large-scale change happens through people. And people skills are what STEM professionals are often least known for, if not outright criticized for.

In 2005, the National Academies of Science published "Educating the Engineer of 2020: Adapting Engineering Education to the New Century." More than a decade later, very little has changed. For most STEM educators, the question "what should education be like today and in the future?" is still unanswered.

There is no shortage of academic rigor in the technical preparation of STEM students. However, it is clear that industry expects STEM professionals to excel in both technical and nontechnical skills (people skills). And for good reason: STEM disciplines are driving societal change. These fields create innovations that are brought to market and change human behavior, lifestyle, health, well-being, and (in general) our day-to-day living. The need for innovation is significant since the globe faces no shortage of challenges—everything from climate change to energy crises to cybersecurity. There is no time more crucial than now for STEM professionals to combine their expertise with wisdom. The risks of not having the skills to work with and manage people include innovation for the sake of innovation and slow progress on changes society needed yesterday. These risks are too high to ignore and to leave unresolved.

Your work as a STEM professional directly improves society by the problems you choose to solve, the products you make, and the processes you refine. This line of work faces great expectations from organizations and society. But those expectations feel, at times, unrealistic because the people who benefit the most from your work don't actually know what, exactly, you do on a day-to-day basis.

Unfortunately, while technical skills are adequately taught in the best colleges worldwide, individuals are left to figure out nontechnical skills on their own or through on-the-job experiences. Nontechnical skills include everything that has to do with interacting with people. Charting these rarely navigated waters is challenging, especially considering the perfection-oriented standards in STEM fields. And in addition to the pressure to perform perfectly, ethical quandaries accompany every problem that needs to be solved. Developing these skills may cause enormous stress because organizations seldom offer nontechnical skill training focused on technical employees. Instead, training is often done in the form of on-the-job feedback, in which the critique will impact your reputation. And yet, even without a formal leadership title or with underdeveloped nontechnical skills, STEM professionals are viewed as leaders when challenging situations arise because they are considered the go-to problem solvers.

Think of the Fibonacci sequence, one of the most famous formulas in mathematics. The formula shows that each number in the sequence is the sum of the two numbers that precede it. Thus, the sequence goes: 0, 1, 1, 2, 3, 5, 8, 13, 21, and so on.

Like the Fibonacci sequence, STEM responsibilities start relatively small. Perhaps you're overseeing product management or contributing to the analysis of research study data. But then, as each assignment is completed, the tasks get more extensive and so do the responsibilities and pressure. With the advancement of technology, science, health care, and society, the trajectory of complexity, accountability, and tension grows infinitely, like the Fibonacci formula. There's no doubt that STEM professionals need to become equally skilled in both the technical and nontechnical aspects of their roles to be effective professionals that make a difference.

This guide aims to be an often-used reference that will be found on the desk of any STEM professional or student, across fields, industries, and levels. With each part, we add a new layer of complexity to working with others. We start with part 1, "The First Principle Is You," and end with part 5, "The First Principles of Leading Teams of Teams." Each topic in each part follows a consistent structure so you know what to expect when you flip through and find a problem you're trying to solve or a capability you're trying to improve upon.

- We start with naming and introducing problems you might identify with or encounter in your day-to-day activities.

- We then share a concept taken from the field of organization development, which is a leading field that integrates social psychology theory with business theory.

- We follow with a section called "Putting the Concept into Practice," which offers methods and tips to act as your tool kit for addressing the problem.

- We then offer a metaphor from the STEM fields to help make sense of the social concepts and methods.

- To wrap up, we include reflection questions to encourage you to pause and see how the content resonates with you and how you might use this information to develop your skills.

- Finally, the last subheading provides references and further reading, if you're intrigued by any of the concepts.

We recognize that it is challenging to incorporate all the content we present in this book all at once—so don't! You might read it front to back and gradually incorporate the material into your integral self in a natural progression from self to leading others. Or, you might wait until you have a problem that needs fixing and flip to the topic that helps you the most. Use the table of contents and headings to help guide you to what you need in the moment.

For you to effectively use this guide, we suggest bringing an open mind and pushing yourself to be bold and honest with your self-evaluations. Nontechnical skills are not about validity, certainty, and predictions. They are about changing and choosing the paradigms of thinking that most of use to help us navigate complex systems and complex humans simultaneously.

We do encourage you to focus on using this guide for yourself and not for the purpose of fixing others. And even though it might be tempting, we encourage you not to argue against the content in this book or try to solve it as a problem. Instead, try to constantly connect it back to you personally and think about how it might help you. Seek to find at least one idea in the moment that you find helpful. Identify a new way of thinking that might be worth a try.

And now we, the authors, would like to share a word about our process and our passion. Both of us have deep experience in the STEM industry and in organization development. Crystal studied as a chemical engineer and worked in manufacturing before taking up the challenge of solving people problems and maximizing human potential in the field of organization development. Janette studied cognitive science, international business, and psychology, and she served as the interim executive director at the Bernard Gordon Engineering Leadership Center at the Jacobs School of Engineering.

In our experience, STEM professionals are often described as not being able to effectively navigate the interpersonal dynamics of professional relationships. And we felt strongly that this reputation was not deserved—many STEM professionals haven't had the opportunity to develop such capabilities and are judged unfairly for this lack of development. We also noticed the impact of STEM fields, and we saw how exceptional STEM professionals work hard to become masters of both technical and nontechnical skills.

We wrote this book 100 percent virtually and have never met in person. We had our own challenges navigating the very problems we have written about here. What we have learned is that it is possible to grow these nontechnical capabilities, whether you are just starting your professional journey or are an experienced professional.

We hope you find that this guide helps puts words to the emotions, dynamics, and situations you experience and, as a result, helps you act more effectively. We hope this guide empowers you to do your technical work while keeping an eye on the broader implications of your work for society—both your internal work relationships and external societal customers. With help from this guide, you should become able to intelligently and influentially express yourself in every communication, not simply offer the technical answers. We look forward to your growth as a socially responsible leader—the next step in your development as a technical professional.

PART 1

N = x

THE FIRST PRINCIPLE IS YOU

After hearing others share innovative practices, a director replied, "Don't be fooled by these practices. They are important, but they are a consequence, not the cause. Of our sixty managers, we have five or six that no matter where I assign them, they build units that achieve extraordinary performance."

One of my colleagues asked, "What do they do?"

There was a long silence. The director said, "That is the wrong question. It is not because of what they do; it is about who they are."

—**ROBERT QUINN,** paraphrased from
Building the Bridge as You Walk On It

STEM professionals like you are responsible for driving some of the most impactful innovations of our time. And what you spend your time thinking about impacts you, those around you, and the solutions you create together. Most of your education has probably focused on building technical skills. You have the basic capability that served as the table stakes that got you in the door to start working. What makes the difference with your success is who you are.

This may be the first time you are considering who you are as an important part of your self-development journey. Instead of viewing others as the problem that needs fixing on the way to successful outcomes, we need to start by looking at ourselves. Often, the most complex challenge is admitting that we are part of the problems we see—and yet, the one person we can realistically control is ourselves. The first step in becoming a STEM professional who effectively leads change is to lead yourself well. This is the foundation for all other skills that involve working with others. Because of the importance of this skill, you may find yourself repeatedly returning to this part.

CONNECT BACK TO WHY

Steve Jobs once said, "A lot of people in our industry haven't had very diverse experiences. So, they don't have enough dots to connect, and they end up with very linear solutions without a broad perspective on the problem. The broader one's understanding of the human experience, the better design we will have."[1] Learning about yourself—and your limits in perspective—helps you reduce bias in your work. By reducing bias, you will be able to create more inclusive solutions that affect society positively.

You might be wondering, where has my education been for diving into myself? In this first part, we will explore the following ways to gain insights about yourself:

- **GROWING SELF-AWARENESS (PAGE 5):** Use the concept of the Johari Window to learn what exactly you do and don't know about yourself.

- **MANAGING YOUR REACTIONS (PAGE 16):** Learn what guides instant, often ineffective, reactions—especially reactions rooted in the Four Fatal Fears.

- **PAUSING AND CREATING SPACE (PAGE 26):** Learn how to develop your ability to be mindful and to wait before reacting—this allows us to stop the burnout-causing cycle of doing and reacting.

- **THINKING BEYOND PROBLEMS, NEGATIVITY, AND DEFICIENCIES (PAGE 35):** Learn that it's okay to move beyond your problem-solving "what's not working" mindset and that there is more inspiration and positive action to gain by adding Appreciative Inquiry to your mindset.

- **MAKING DECISIONS AND TAKING ACTION (PAGE 46):** Learn about the shortcuts or heuristics we use that do not serve rational decision-making and how perspective-taking can help.

1.1

GROWING YOUR SELF-AWARENESS | THE JOHARI WINDOW

Our personal myths blind us to knowing what we can and can't do. Seeing who we are in this moment—our health, our motivation, the messages coming from our world—gives us the information we need to continue on.

[Yet], the maps we need are in us, but not in only one of us. If we read the currents and signs together, we'll find our way through.

—**MARGARET WHEATLEY,** *Perseverance*

THE PROBLEM These are just *some* of the problems you might encounter that growing your self-awareness helps solve.	• Do you feel like you're often running on autopilot, choosing the same reactions, and not adjusting in the moment to the situation? • Do you clash with others easily? • Have you received feedback that you're not coachable? • Do you struggle with imposter syndrome or self-esteem? • Do you feel progress isn't happening as often as usual in certain situations or with certain people?

No one knows you better than you know yourself. But, ironically, you don't know your whole self effortlessly—it requires intention and work. It's a natural outcome of living as a complex being, taking in and interpreting many types and quantities of data every second. That's why the depth at which we *consciously* know our character, feelings, and motives widely varies among individuals. And, just like any good system, we can act our best in present moments when we are thoughtfully acting based on our complete data set, rather than reacting based on past data or other preprogramming residing in our brains. As Margaret Wheatley says, "When we are overwhelmed and confused, our brains barely function. We reach for the old maps, the routine responses, what worked in the past."[2]

The level that we know ourselves comes from calling attention to the different aspects that make us who we are. Calling attention to these various aspects is called building self-awareness. There are two aspects of self-awareness, internal and external.

- **INTERNAL SELF-AWARENESS:** Focuses on consciously understanding and surfacing our individual core beliefs, values, and attitudes.

- **EXTERNAL SELF-AWARENESS:** Helps us understand how these core beliefs, values, and attributes impact others.

Although both are equally important, you must first grow your internal self-awareness to evaluate your impact accurately and build external self-awareness. In this topic, we share the concept of the Johari Window, which will help you take the first step.

GROWING YOUR SELF-AWARENESS BY EXPLORING THE JOHARI WINDOW

In every human interaction, there is an element of mystery. Why? We are different, one from another, but everyone knows something that no one else knows. To add to the drama, each of us lacks awareness of certain aspects of our own behavior or feelings which others can clearly see.

—JOSEPH LUFT, "The Johari Window"

The Johari Window is a model developed by Joseph Luft and Harry Ingham to help guide self-awareness and interpersonal interactions.[3] They called it a window because the model looks like a windowpane with four squares.

The Open and Hidden squares signify internal self-awareness. The Open and Blind squares signify information shared with others, whether intentionally or unintentionally. The Blind and Unknown squares signify information about ourselves that we are unaware of and are in our external self-awareness. The Hidden square is information that we know about ourselves but do not share with others, and the Unknown square signifies information that neither we nor others are aware of.

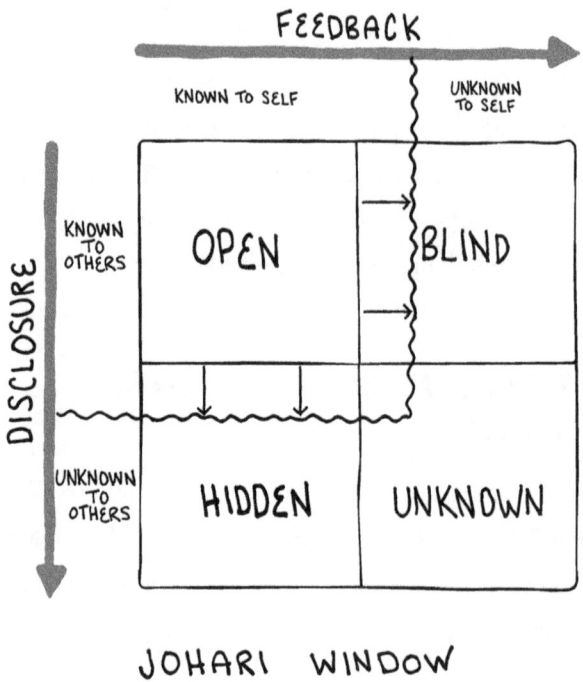

JOHARI WINDOW

1. **THE OPEN SQUARE (INTERNAL SELF-AWARENESS):** This information about yourself is disclosed openly—it is both clearly known by self and known by others. We can think of square one as the level of information we feel comfortable sharing on social media, with coworkers, or with casual friends. The data is truly open-source.

2. **THE HIDDEN SQUARE (INTERNAL SELF-AWARENESS):** This is information you know about yourself that you do not

share with others. The Hidden area represents the boundary where you stop disclosing information about yourself to others. We feel vulnerable sharing in the Hidden area and disclose information only to those we know well and trust. Often, in the moment, you reflect on what you know and feel and consider what and with whom you are willing to share that knowledge with.

3. **THE BLIND SQUARE (EXTERNAL SELF-AWARENESS):** This information about you is known by others but unknown to you. Ever feel like something is obvious to everyone else, but you are too close to the fire to see it? We can be blind to our impact on others, and without knowing it, their reactions might drive us to act a particular way. And since we haven't discovered and integrated that data with our internal self-awareness, we can form unconscious biases, which may be apparent to others but not ourselves.

4. **THE UNKNOWN SQUARE (EXTERNAL SELF-AWARENESS):** This is information about yourself that is unknown to you and unknown to others. In other words, there is a lot that we don't know we don't know that others also don't know! As you go through life, you are getting new data all the time, and there is always more to process and integrate into your self-awareness. We might be afraid of what we might find, we might worry about unlocking emotions or sharing what we don't know that we don't know with others. However, the rewards of increased self-discovery and the ability to thoughtfully act based on new self-awareness are worth it.

NETFLIX JOHARI WINDOW

SERIES THAT YOU AND YOUR FRIEND WATCHED	SERIES THAT YOUR FRIEND WATCHED (YOU DIDN'T)
SERIES THAT YOU WATCHED (YOUR FRIEND DIDN'T)	SERIES NEITHER OF YOU HAVE WATCHED

The size of these squares, or windows, are not equal and unchanging. They change dynamically as you grow your self-awareness. The level of feedback you are willing to receive and the level of self-disclosure you engage in drive how big the panes of your window are.

Your goal is to widen the Open square by being willing to hear feedback and by disclosing information about yourself as appropriate.

A STEM METAPHOR TO DRIVE THE POINT HOME: THE CYNEFIN FRAMEWORK

If you're still confused, here's an analogous concept from the STEM world that might help. A practical framework to explore the content and context of situations is called the Cynefin framework.[4] The model has four domains, each requiring a different set of actions: simple, complicated, complex, and chaotic.

- The simple domain involves situations with repeated patterns and consistent events with a predictable outcome. The simple process to follow in this domain is to sense, categorize, and then respond to known knowns.

- The second domain is complicated situations. In the complicated domain, an expert's opinion is needed. For example, when a check engine light in your car comes on, you take your car to a mechanic to find out what is wrong. The process followed is this: sense, analyze, and then respond to known unknowns.

- The third domain is complex. Situations in the complex domain are in constant flux and unpredictable. The process followed is this: probe first, then sense, and then respond to the unknown unknowns.

- The fourth domain is chaotic. The immediate response is to act, sense, and respond to the unknowable.

We live in an ever-changing environment where many knowns and unknowns about ourselves, others, and the contexts of situations continually emerge. To grow internal self-awareness and learn about external self-awareness, we need to consciously know what we know and then seek to understand what we don't know.

A STORY IN ACTION

In a recent meeting, Marquez presented his ideas to the team. Skye, a colleague, joined the meeting late. She interrupted the flow of the conversation by jumping in and asking, "Hey, what are we discussing?"

Against Marquez's wishes, he stopped the meeting to bring Skye up to speed so he could get back to the presentation. As Marquez was giving the CliffsNotes version, Skye kept asking follow-up questions that had already been discussed.

After the meeting, Marquez privately spoke with Skye to share the impact she had on him by being late to the meeting. Skye sincerely apologized for being late. And she added that she felt she could make up for being late to the meeting by participating and asking questions.

As a result of getting feedback, Skye could see a blind area (i.e., known to others and unknown to her). Marquez also learned something about himself. He decided that the next time someone arrives late to a meeting, he will say, "In the interest of time, we can catch you up offline—perhaps someone is willing to share their notes?" and he will assign that role as needed.

PUTTING THE CONCEPT INTO PRACTICE

How can you apply the Johari Window to your life? Seeking to widen and expand your Open window is a healthy goal. It indicates a desire for conscious behavior and sets the stage for healthy relationships with others and with yourself.

Some techniques you can use to intentionally widen your Open window are covered here. But since self-awareness is a fundamental skill, we will build on these techniques in later topics.

- **PAUSE AND CONSIDER DISCLOSURE TO REDUCE THE HIDDEN WINDOW:** Sometimes trust issues, conflicts, misunderstandings, and miscommunications happen because we aren't disclosing enough about where we are coming from. If you find yourself in this situation, consider whether disclosing might help move a relationship—even ones that you might not trust—forward.

- **ASK FOR FEEDBACK TO REDUCE THE BLIND WINDOW:** To reduce the gap between what is known by others and unknown by us, we can ask for feedback. An example of a blind moment could be repeatedly saying "okay" when someone else is speaking. You might be saying "okay" to affirm you are tracking and listening to what they are saying, but the speaker might think you are saying "okay" because you already know the information. You might learn of this disparity because you notice they tend to cut off explanations abruptly, or they candidly ask you if you have any questions. Or you might even have asked for feedback directly on your communication skills. Asking for feedback grows our external self-awareness exponentially.

- **REFLECT ON THE PRESENT DATA TO REDUCE THE UNKNOWN WINDOW:** Remember what we shared in the introduction about being on autopilot? We repeat old patterns when we don't reflect on the data present in the here and now. Be intentional about taking time in your life, regularly and at significant moments of transition, to reflect on your core beliefs, values, and attributes. Has anything changed from before? What's driving you the most right now? What new data has come to the scene? What feels unknown to you? Are there others who have been in a similar situation who could help you explore your feelings about it? Be open to exploring your Unknown square.

REFLECTION QUESTIONS

- Draw a Johari Window and play around with the size of each square. Make an estimation: What represents the size of each window for yourself right now? Which windows would you like to widen and expand? How might you do that?

- What are some of the core values and beliefs that drive you when it comes to your work? To your relationships? If you're struggling, try filling in the blanks to statements such as "Workstyle ought to be . . . ," "Positive relationships ought to be . . . ," "Communication ought to be . . ." Start noting these as a part of your Open window.

- Have you been in a situation where you recently felt triggered by someone and didn't know why? Take a moment to reflect on the event—did they violate some of the values or beliefs in the previous question? Could this awareness help you communicate and disclose where you were coming from or a need you have?

- Is there a part of your life where you don't get the reaction you would like or where progress forward doesn't happen quickly? These are all signs of lower effectiveness due to a lack of self-awareness. Consider from whom you might ask for feedback and what you would ask them.

FURTHER READING AND REFERENCES

On the more casual side . . . books and resources to check out:

Wheatley, Margaret. (2006). *Leadership and the New Science: Discovering Order in a Chaotic World.*

Wheatley, Margaret. (2010). *Perseverance.*

On the more academic side . . . references we used:

Luft, Joseph, and Harrington Ingham. (1961). "The Johari Window: A Graphic Model of Awareness in Interpersonal Relations."

Snowden, Dave J., and M. E. Boone. (2007). "A Leader's Framework for Decision Making." *Harvard Business Review.*

1.2

MANAGING YOUR REACTIONS | THE FOUR FATAL FEARS

It's the little moments that trigger some of our most outsized and unproductive responses. The more aware we are, the less likely any trigger, even in the most mundane circumstances, will prompt hasty unthinking behavior that leads to undesirable consequences.

—MARSHALL GOLDSMITH, *Triggers*

THE PROBLEM These are just *some* of the problems you might encounter that managing your reactions helps solve.	• Do you notice that you tend to react instantly ... and sometimes regret it later? • Do you notice your relationships have difficulty lasting? • Do you sense that you're doing something to unconsciously harm your team's progress or a relationship? • Do you express emotional and solid responses or stances that make it difficult for others to respond or connect with you?

When we develop our self-awareness, we have a greater ability to choose our reactions. As the saying goes, "Fate is the hand of cards we've been dealt. Choice is how we play the hand."

We can't control what others say or do, but each of us is responsible for the reaction we bring to a situation. Have you ever said or done something that you instantly (or a while later) realized might not have been the best approach? Do your relationships at work sometimes turn out differently than you wanted or feel bumpy? Do you feel uncertain about how to work within a team effectively?

It is instinctual to find someone else to blame and to stick with your approach. Instead, as we shared in the last topic, you are more effective when you are aware of the beliefs, values, and attitudes that drove you in a particular situation. This self-awareness can guide you the next time a similar trigger pops up. Or you can reflect, learn, and go back and try communicating again about the topic that triggered you.

How do you grow your self-awareness and figure out what drove your reaction? We'll build on the Johari Window concept with a new concept, the Four Fatal Fears, to develop your ability to pause and choose your responses in the moment.

MANAGING YOUR REACTIONS BY CONSIDERING THE FOUR FATAL FEARS

Emotions often guide our reactions. Emotions are intense feelings associated with a specific event. The brain relies on past experiences to predict and make sense of an event. Particularly extreme events can elicit intense emotions that can linger through the creation of long-lasting neural maps or in your body in places that remain tight or tense, even after the event has passed.

For example, say you recently interviewed for a new job. You felt you did well, but the organization selected another candidate. This news causes the brain to recall past times when you were sad, mad, or disappointed. Your body may get tense as you recollect these memories. These emotions may linger for a few minutes, but after a short time, the brain will switch to processing new incoming information, and the cycle will start all over again.

This fast-processing cycle, which is based on the past and not necessarily wholly accurate or aligned with the present, is often at the root of ineffective reactions. In the moment, we might not know what we don't know about ourselves and therefore we might be operating in the Blind or Unknown areas of the Johari Window. Or we might know what's going on but aren't ready to communicate it (the Hidden area of the Johari Window).

To manage reactions more effectively, we need a way to start naming our emotions and moving them to the Open area of the Johari Window so we can deal with them consciously. One of the strongest emotions that creates ineffective and often defensive reactions is fear.

To get perspective and expand your Open window, you can consider whether the Four Fatal Fears are at play.[5] Maxie Maultsby, Jr., a psychiatrist specializing in emotional and behavioral self-management, believes that the Four Fatal Fears consciously and unconsciously influence our attitudes: rejection, failure, discomfort, and being wrong.

Managing Your Reactions | The Four Fatal Fears | 19

- **FEAR OF REJECTION:** Humans are social beings with a strong desire to be accepted. The fear of *rejection* can hinder us from getting to know others and allowing others to get to know us. We might struggle with self-disclosure and keep more in our Hidden window. When reacting based on this fear, we are saying, "I need to be accepted." Sometimes, this expression can happen positively, but it can often manifest as anxious, needy, or otherwise negative behavior.

- **FEAR OF FAILURE:** The fear of *failure* of a product or research study and the need for success couldn't be more relevant to a STEM professional. Technical professions experience enormous pressure to create breakthrough ideas, processes, and solutions in record time. When reacting based on the fear of failure, you are primarily being driven by the thought "I need to succeed." Despite the urgency in the situation, you might express a lot of caution, create a lot of checkpoints, and be perceived as the roadblock when you try to guard against fear of failure.

- **FEAR OF EMOTIONAL DISCOMFORT:** The fear of dealing with or having negative emotions either within yourself or shared by others is the fear of *emotional discomfort*. The more you practice being uncomfortable, the more you will become familiar with the feeling, and this will allow you to be more emotionally stable in such situations. Emotional stability is a person's ability to withstand high levels of stress. When you have a low level of emotional stability, you are often driven by the thought "I need to maintain comfort and safety for myself." You might try to make jokes to lighten the situation, fail to show appropriate empathy, or use other self-protective measures to avoid emotional discomfort rather than engaging with it.

- **FEAR OF BEING WRONG:** The need to appear to know everything and be right is often a problem for technical professionals. Individuals in STEM careers often pride themselves on having the answer and are often rewarded for it. Instead of admitting what you don't know or that alternative points of view might also be right when you fear being wrong, you are often driven by a need for your way to be the right way. You might make others feel wrong in the process—even if there is no clear right answer—which can significantly affect your working relationships. Remember that you also have a Blind window, where you don't know things that others might know. Also, remember that problems in your professional life are complex; multiple points of view could be correct, but they may simply address different parts of a situation.

These Four Fatal Fears can drive many ineffective reactions. In the "Putting the Concept into Practice" section, we will share how to pause and choose a different path instead of reacting.

A STEM METAPHOR TO DRIVE THE POINT HOME: NEWTON'S THIRD LAW

In Newtonian physics, there is an equal and opposite reaction for every action. But we are not static, physical objects—we are human beings who are complex and dynamic. What we can control and influence is *what* the reaction is, *how* equal the reaction is, and our interpretations of what is appropriate.

When we react, we tend to react to the action happening now and what actions have happened to us in the past. When we have a negative reaction, the size of our reaction is often based on fears—fears about the present, fears about things from the past that help protect us now and in the future, and fears generated by imagined predictions of the future.

Instead of reacting, it would be great if we could have a purposeful response. We want to pause and have a reaction that is equal and appropriate to the action that has taken place.

A STORY IN ACTION

Miya was asked to take the lead as the product manager for the new product line. Her boss and coworkers felt she would do a terrific job because she was a resourceful team player.

A few months into the process, some issues with the manufacturer's supply chain started to impact the product launch timeline. In the past, Miya was always able to make magic happen, which had impressed her boss and coworkers. But this time her magic was not working.

The fear of failure started to creep into Miya's thoughts. Miya became increasingly anxious, and that showed up in meetings as impatience, frustration, and badgering others to overcome barriers. Furthermore, her need to appear strong and her fear of emotional discomfort grew as the project and its expected schedule unraveled. Her usual strengths of agility and creative thinking felt impossible to regain, but she pushed any idea she could come up with. She started to second-guess herself.

Miya took a moment to pause. In a moment of clarity, she reflected on a past occasion when one of her coworkers, Antonio, had been in dire straits and had leveraged his network for help. Antonio's willingness to self-disclose (tell—Hidden area) about his situation empowered Miya to reach out and help. Additionally, Antonio had asked Miya for feedback on what he was missing (Blind area), which strengthened the relationship between Miya and Antonio.

After reflecting on Antonio's experience and her own situation, Miya decided she couldn't hold it in any longer and told the team about the fears she was experiencing. As a result, she learned that one of her peers knew someone else who worked for the manufacturer. He was able to call in a favor and get a meeting. Miya was then able to use her magic and creativity on the call to get the supplies back on schedule. Miya and the team were back in business, and the timeline was back on track. Miya's only regret in the process was not sharing with her team earlier.

PUTTING THE CONCEPT INTO PRACTICE

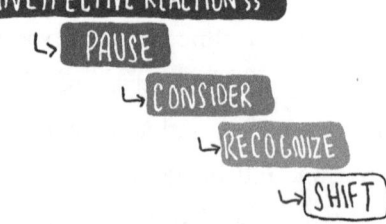

How can you apply the Four Fatal Fears to manage your reactions? Here are a few steps that you can take:

1. Realize you are in the midst of or about to have an ineffective reaction.

2. Pause—even if you think it's too late. It's never too late to backtrack. Don't be afraid to take a moment away from the conversation if you need to. Just say something along the lines of, "Let me take a moment to reflect and get grounded, and then we can proceed."

3. During your pause, consider what role fear is playing. Which one or more of the Four Fatal Fears is driving you?

4. Recognize that your fatal fear(s) are creating their own goal for the moment. Refocus on the mutual goal—what is the shared goal?

5. Shift your reaction. You can simply say, "Let me take a step back." And then consider one or more of the following pathways:

    a. Share your fear with others so you can find a mutually beneficial solution together.

    b. If you have a mutually beneficial solution in mind that quells your fear and moves the group forward, share it.

    c. Take a longer pause, consider staying in silence/observation mode until you have had more time to process, and then come back more effectively later on.

Remember that these Four Fatal Fears apply to everyone—not just you! In a certain situation, you might be reacting out of one fear and your teammates, another! Henry Ford said, " . . . whether you think you can or you think you can't, you're right."[6] We might not always identify with our emotions, but research shows that all of us have feelings that manifest as a result of our brains' predictions about every given situation. It's important to manage our reactions to respond effectively to the present situation and data.

REFLECTION QUESTIONS

- What current situations have you had that created an emotional reaction?

- When you reflect on that situation, what emotions do you remember experiencing?

- How did you handle the situation?

- Which of the Four Fatal Fears do you feel like you deal with often?

- Where do you think this comes from?

- What might help you cope with your fatal fears?

FURTHER READING AND REFERENCES

On the more casual side . . . books and resources to check out:

Goldsmith, Marshall. (2015). *Triggers: Creating Behavior That Lasts—Becoming the Person You Want to Be.*

Wilson, Larry, and Hersch Wilson. (2004). *Play to Win: Choosing Growth Over Fear in Work and Life.*

1.3

PAUSING AND CREATING SPACE | MINDFULNESS

People don't understand that the hardest thing is actually doing something that is close to nothing. It demands all of you . . . there is no object to hide behind. It's just you.

—**MARINA ABRAMOVIĆ,** artist, as quoted in *Stillness Is the Key* by Ryan Holiday

THE PROBLEM These are just *some* problems you might encounter that pausing and creating space help solve.	• Do you struggle with instantly reacting rather than thinking and then acting or speaking? • Do you feel overwhelmed and crave more internal space? • Do you feel burned out? • Do you want to break through running on autopilot and move towards becoming more intentional? • Do you want to feel like you have a choice and choose your path forward most of the time?

Did you know our brains process six to seven thousand thoughts daily?[7] Most of those thoughts happen so quickly that we cannot fully process them. Until we become conscious of our thoughts, although we might believe we are "thinking," in reality, we are engaged in subconscious processing.

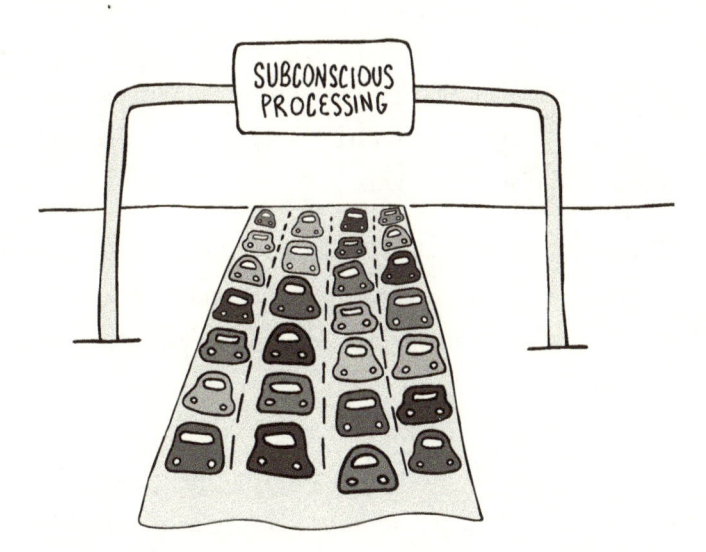

As we shared in the previous topics, we are constantly acting and reacting to life. We may consciously choose our actions or be prompted to react by our subconscious mind. The goal is to grow our self-awareness and choose our actions to perform our jobs with greater insights about ourselves, about others, and about the collaborative process. If we are not driving towards conscious processing, we will be likely to experience the following challenges:

- **WE BECOME DISTRACTED AND LESS PRODUCTIVE:** Our brain chatter distracts us from what we want to pay attention to. Even though we might believe we are focused, our effort is probably pointing us in unproductive directions.

- **WE FEEL OVERWHELMED:** We can't see the bigger picture (or the forest) because all the minute details (or trees) get in the way.

- **WE FIND OURSELVES ON AUTOPILOT OR BURNED OUT:** All we can manage to do is react to incoming data and people and just try to keep up.

- **WE DON'T FEEL STRATEGIC:** We lose sight of the purpose we are trying to achieve and don't have the capacity to put together an intentional plan to get there.

- **WE OVERLOOK OUR IMPACT ON OTHERS:** Our relationships and team dynamics suffer because we are not thinking about what will help us and our teams move forward in a positive, generative direction.

Remember, you're at work because your perspective, expertise, interpretation, and solutions are needed. You're at your most valuable when you are not reacting on autopilot or repeating ideas already out there. The first step in regaining intentionality and conscious action is to take a step back. Developing *mindfulness* as a core capability allows you to *master the pause*.

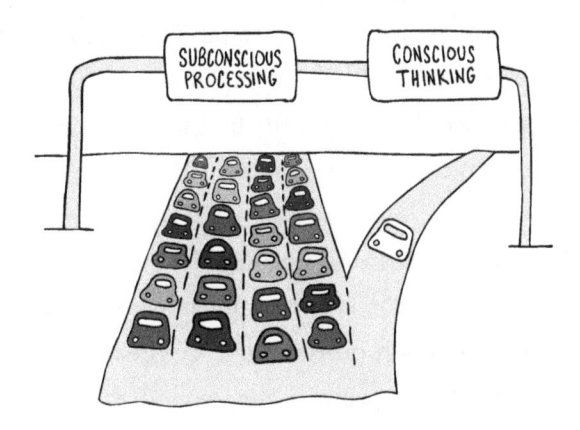

PAUSING AND CREATING SPACE THROUGH MINDFULNESS

Mindfulness is an awareness cultivated by paying attention in a sustained and particular way: on purpose, in the present moment, and nonjudgmentally.[8] Consider that spending time in a mindful state allows you to self-source wisdom and insights, rather than outsourcing that brilliance to someone else or crowdsourcing brilliance from external sources. Mindfulness will enable you to know what you think and to form your own unique point of view, rather than focusing on what everyone else is telling you to think.

Mindfulness is about pausing to acknowledge the moment we are in and stepping back from the overwhelming stream of thoughts that distract us. As explained by Wendy Tan, "Clearing is emptying our mental clutter, judgments, and emotions, and being whole in the moment. This void allows us to receive new ideas and connect to when, who, and what matters most."[9] Mindfulness allows our consciousness to catch up with our subconscious. By pausing periodically, we become more aware of ourselves and our context. This pause to take time and be present in the moment creates an important gap of time between our thoughts and our actions. It gives us a chance to respond rather than react.

Whether you're trying to expand your Johari Window or address a Fatal Fear, you can use mindfulness to take that pause. Neuroscience and psychology expert David Rock explains that focusing on your immediate experiences helps calm the limbic system, which is largely responsible for distractions:

> We talk about stopping and smelling the roses. . . . If you can spend a whole ten seconds just completely taking in the data, focusing your attention on the different streams of data, the depth of the smell, the quality of the smell, all that—and not so much the story of it. This is the neuroscience of mindfulness.[10]

Developing your mindfulness capability is essential if you want to truly grow your self-awareness, manage your reactions, and become a professional who is not just technically competent but also able to work with others to make a positive difference. As Ryan Holiday puts it in his book *Stillness Is the Key*, "To be steady while the world spins around you. To act without frenzy. It's all but impossible to find a philosophical school or religion that does not venerate this inner peace—this stillness—as the highest good and as the key to elite performance and a happy life. And when all the wisdom of the ancient world agrees on something, only a fool would decline to listen."[11]

The deliberate actions that create space for discovering your purpose or intention are important and should not be skipped. In the "Putting the Concept into Practice" section, we explain the steps to follow to start developing your mindfulness capability.

A STEM METAPHOR TO DRIVE THE POINT HOME: MAKING TRADE-OFFS

In all technical work, there are trade-offs. At the start of a project, input volume needs to be prioritized to determine what gets included and excluded. Deciphering trade-offs early will set the project up for optimal solutions and success. Conversely, not deciphering trade-offs early can reduce the likelihood of finding the optimal solutions.

This concept of trade-offs also applies to our thoughts and our working capacity to hold those thoughts. We trade strategic thinking for mindless reactions when we allow the stream of thoughts to continue without mindfulness.

A STORY IN ACTION

Destiny came to Yoon's office, hoping to share important information about what is happening in her personal life and how it affects her work. Destiny arrived while Yoon was in the middle of responding to an email from her boss, but Yoon welcomed Destiny in anyway.

Yoon asked Destiny, "What's on your mind?"

As Destiny shared her personal details, Yoon felt distracted the entire time. She was still thinking about how she would finish responding to her boss's email. Although Yoon appeared to listen to Destiny and nodded a few times, she only caught pieces of information.

Destiny finished speaking and waited for Yoon to respond to what she had just shared. To Destiny's surprise, Yoon simply said, "Sounds good, we can make that happen."

Destiny had a strange look on her face and slowly got up and left. After Destiny walked out, Yoon suddenly realized that she didn't hear most of what Destiny said and that she had dismissed Destiny by responding with a ready-made statement. And Yoon wasn't sure what she had missed.

She was so distracted by the email, her anxiety, and how to reply that she couldn't focus. In the aftermath of the conversation with Destiny, Yoon didn't know whether Destiny would feel safe approaching her again in the future. She would have to try again to see what Destiny needed.

If Yoon had taken a moment to draw a deep breath and close her laptop or browser window, she would have been able to tap into a mindful state and become more present. Yoon needs to learn how these small physical actions can allow her to quiet her inner world.

PUTTING THE CONCEPT INTO PRACTICE

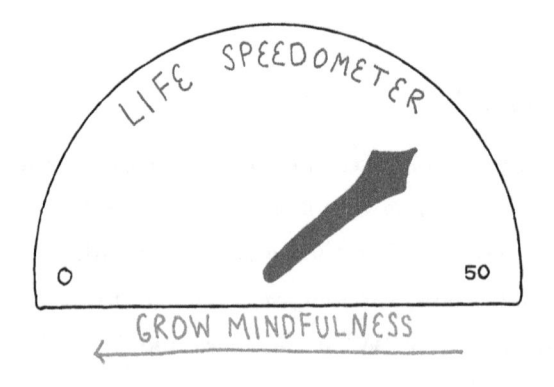

LIFE SPEEDOMETER

0   50

← GROW MINDFULNESS

It might be hard to go from zero to one hundred, from no practice to daily yoga or breathing practice, to become more mindful!

Let's consider some small steps to help grow mindfulness instead.

1. If you're feeling any of the challenges named in the introduction, use that as a cue that it is time for you to step back and become more mindful of what is going on with you.

2. Focus on your present environment for a moment. What do you experience with your five senses; what do you see, feel,

smell, hear, and taste? Give your limbic system a moment to quiet down.

3. Then turn your attention to your stream of thoughts. Don't try to stop the thoughts. Instead, give yourself a moment to simply notice them. What are they?

4. Write the thoughts down. Often, you can "name it to tame it" when it comes to anxiety, overwhelm, distraction, or other emotions. By writing thoughts down, you honor them, so you don't have to hold them in your memory and allow them to take up some of your brain capacity. Use whatever mechanism helps you get the thoughts out. If journaling isn't your thing, consider recording a voice note to yourself, drawing a mind-map,[12] or using another means to express your thoughts.

5. Do you see any themes? What is emerging as the problem? What action or goal would you prefer instead? What might you need? What intentional desired path forward is coming up when you clear and create space for your thoughts?

REFLECTION QUESTIONS

- How have you practiced stepping back and being mindful in the past?
- How do you think being more mindful could help you?
- What do you do to stay focused and in the present?
- How do you handle the situation when you get interrupted by people, thoughts, and technology?

FURTHER READING AND REFERENCES

On the more casual side . . . books and resources to check out:

Holiday, Ryan. (2019). *Stillness Is the Key*.

Mindmapping. https://www.mindmapping.com.

Tan, Wendy. (2017). *Wholeness in a Disruptive World: Pearls of Wisdom from East and West*.

Rosier, Rich. (2011). "A Conversation with David Rock on Self-Regulation and Leadership." Linkage. https://www.linkageinc.com/leadership-insights/a-conversation-with-david-rock-on-self-regulation-and-leadership.

On the more academic side . . . references we used:

Kabat-Zinn, J. (1994). *Mindfulness Meditation for Everyday Life*.

Tseng, J., and J. Poppenk. (2020). "Brain Meta-State Transitions Demarcate Thoughts across Task Contexts Exposing the Mental Noise of Trait Neuroticism." *Nature Communications*. https://doi.org/10.1038/s41467-020-17255-9.

1.4

THINKING BEYOND PROBLEMS, NEGATIVITY, AND DEFICIENCIES | APPRECIATIVE INQUIRY

It all starts with inquiry. The seeds of change are implicit in the very first questions we ask! The questions we ask, the things that we choose to focus on, the topics that we choose determine what we find. Inquiry is intervention.

—DAVID COOPERRIDER, *Introduction to Appreciative Inquiry*

The practice of Appreciative Inquiry chooses the positive inquiry precisely because it leads to positive images that, in turn, create a positive future.

—WATKINS, MOHR, AND KELLY, *Appreciative Inquiry*

THE PROBLEM These are just *some* of the challenges you might encounter that thinking beyond problems, negativity, and deficiencies helps solve.	• Do you get feedback that you are the pessimist in the room—always bringing up what the team can't do or what is standing in the way? • Do you feel like nothing you do makes a difference and that there are just too many problems to ever achieve anything? • Do you tend to focus solely on the issues and weaknesses in a situation? • Do you want to feel more inspired and craft a positive vision?

Do you ever get the sense that you're seen as the roadblock in the room? That you are the only one who sees the problems and, therefore, has to be the one who solves them? While everyone else might be excited and optimistic, you might be the voice saying "hold on a second" and raising concerns about the risks.

One of the main questions technical individuals tend to ask when facing a situation is: "What problem are we trying to solve?" The rigorous training undertaken by STEM professionals, regardless of the specialization, focuses on making things better; therefore, almost everything is examined through the lens of what is wrong so it can be fixed. Being in a steady state of problem-solving can dim our outlook on situations, people, and even ourselves. It can also make us the least likable person in the room—adding pressure that can trigger the beginning of unhealthy relationships and team culture.

This steady state of problem-solving might initially feel fine. But working day in and day out on problems can have a big impact on you as an individual. Have you ever felt low for a while? Have you ever woken up and felt like the weight of the world is on your shoulders? Have you had a feeling of heaviness or a negative mood but couldn't articulate the cause? Have these feelings gone on for an extended period of time?

This could be you experiencing problem-solving burnout. Burnout, in general, is when you deeply and persistently experience one or all of the following feelings and thoughts: self-doubt, alone or isolated, trapped, increasingly negative outlook, or decreased sense of accomplishment. Burnout at any level inhibits our ability to inspire ourselves and others. So, where does problem-solving burnout come from?

Although it is our job to improve things by finding problems and fixing them constantly, we can balance ourselves by interjecting positive thinking.

Whether you find yourself down for a moment or in a longer-term phase of burnout, positive thinking that sees and leverages what's working helps protect our thinking but still delivers exceptional outcomes.

Positive thinking can be interpreted and applied in many ways. Some people interpret being positive as ignoring the negative and making things sound better than they are. This kind of positive thinking can frustrate technically oriented individuals because it simply doesn't represent the facts of reality. However, positive thinking can also focus on the power of strengths within reality. This concept is called Appreciative Inquiry.

THINKING BEYOND PROBLEMS, NEGATIVITY, AND DEFICIENCIES THROUGH APPRECIATIVE INQUIRY

One way to balance our problem-solving perspective is to combine advocacy (making your case) and inquiry (curiosity).[13]

Advocacy is the primary position STEM professionals take throughout the day. They are expected to figure out what needs to be done, make a case for the solution, enlist people to support the effort, and execute the plan. They are often promoted and rewarded for powerfully debating and influencing others.

However, when advocacy is your primary go-to skill, it can sometimes be counterproductive when working with others, mainly when the situation includes multiple people. You might find yourself constantly reacting to one or more of the Four Fatal Fears, such as the fear of being wrong and defending your need to be right, rather than collaborating or simply being aware of others' expertise. Strong self-advocacy can create a cycle where you feel you are the only one who can solve problems, especially complex ones. In reality, others' thinking may help you shoulder the burden.

The solution to this cycle is an easy and intuitive answer—move from talking to asking. Inquiry skills are helpful when dealing with extreme complexity that requires us to tap into others as resources for insight. How can you move from advocacy to inquiry and especially *Appreciative* Inquiry?

Before we talk about Appreciative Inquiry, let's talk about inquiry in general. A productive way to build skills in inquiry—the art of asking questions—is by cultivating your curiosity. Curiosity naturally arises when you sit, pause, and notice—when you practice mindfulness. Rather than responding to the urgent need to solve the problem as fast as possible, *face* your fear of emotional discomfort (another of those pesky Four Fatal Fears!). Sit with that discomfort and notice the size of the windows in your Johari Window. What might you not know? What you don't know, you don't know.

At first, you might continue you down the problem-solving road with these inquiries. We can ask questions about what's not working all day long (and we often do!). We can beat ourselves up, even though it's not a meaningful use of our time and it's not moving us forward.

Instead, consider building your skills specifically in Appreciative Inquiry. The word *appreciate* in a financial sense means to grow over time. Think of how assets appreciate in value. When you engage in

Appreciative Inquiry, you focus on what is already valuable about a situation and seek to continue to grow that value. As shared in the book *Appreciative Inquiry* by Watkins, Mohr, and Kelly:

> Appreciative Inquiry suggests that by focusing on the deficit, we simply create more images of deficit and potentially overwhelm the system with images of what is "wrong." When we define a situation as a "problem," it means that we have an image of how that situation ought to be—how we'd like it to be. Appreciative Inquiry, on the other hand, looks for what is going "right" and moves towards it, understanding that in the forward movement towards the ideal, the greatest value comes from embracing what works.[14]

FIXING
HOW DO WE FIX THE BROKEN CUPS?

INQUIRY
WHAT FAULT LED TO THE BROKEN CUPS?

APPRECIATIVE INQUIRY
WHAT IS EXCEPTIONAL ABOUT THE BROKEN CUPS? WHAT IF WE MADE THAT THE NORM?
(P.S. THINK OF KINTSUGI)

Given any particular challenge, once you've understood the problem well, Appreciative Inquiry guides you to focus on what strengths everyone and the situation have to solve it. Rather than closing the gap and solving for weaknesses, which takes the team back to where they were, you can be appreciative. In doing so, you may even create a new, better place for the future. In the "Putting the Concept into Practice" section, we will share how you can implement appreciative thinking, in addition to your talent for problem-solving, in your life.

A STEM METAPHOR TO DRIVE THE POINT HOME: VIRAL REACTIONS AND THE FIVE WHYS

A quick analogy for Appreciative Inquiry as a concept is the idea of a viral reaction. Consider how, in viral reactions, what you feed is what grows. If all you do is feed the problems, you will just see more problems! But if you feed your strengths, you grow the strengths to overcome challenges.

A quick analogy for how to go about Appreciative Inquiry is building on the common engineering technique of the five whys or fishbone diagramming for root cause analysis.[15] Consider expanding these investigation techniques from what is not working to what is working and why.

A STORY IN ACTION

Kabir was a highly sought-after engineer because of his skill set and expertise. He was hired recently as a subject matter expert for a large manufacturing company. The job was everything he wanted. Once people learned how technical he was, he quickly became the go-to person for all problems. Daily, Kabir was bombarded with complex issues that were always urgent. After a few months at the company, Kabir started having negative thoughts and moods about the problems he was dealing with and the people who were bringing him the problems. He felt a lot of pressure and responsibility to solve problems and felt fatigued, which made him wonder whether he could maintain the pace and intensity of his work. He found himself looking at everything, including his activities outside of work, as a problem. Relationships at both work and home were starting to be affected by his negative thoughts.

While on a morning run, Kabir reflected on how the job he was so excited about had turned into a negative thing that lived rent-free in his thoughts. He started exploring ways to make problem-solving seem less like a negative thought process.

He recalled some instances in which he felt helpful and energized working with someone who was just as into problem-solving as he was. He felt like he had a thought partner. The person who came to mind was very proactive, assertive, and asked many great questions.

Kabir began to think about how he could leverage other people's strengths. He wondered how he might help others solve their own problems instead of taking them on for them. His thoughts became an inspiring vision for him to try out. Instead of always playing the hero and feeling the pressure, he started picturing a future where he had an army of problem solvers to collaborate with. He was anxious about letting go of the hero image. What if people felt he wasn't trying to help or contribute? But then he stopped himself. He wouldn't know until he tried. Instead, he focused on a curiosity: He wondered whether this approach might change his colleagues' perception of him in ways he couldn't see right now.

Curious about whom he could experiment with, he instantly thought of his new boss. Over the last few months, Kabir's boss, Camila, would check in with him, and he would advocate for what was needed. Often, she didn't agree, and the interaction became a struggle. But now, he would try a different approach with her. He would be more curious about what she wanted to discuss, and he would try to have a more positive interaction with her.

Over the next few weeks, he decided to ask her more questions instead of providing solutions instantly, especially at the beginning of the conversation.

He was amazed at the difference! He found that the more he asked questions and the less he advocated, the more he improved the relationship and the problem-solving process. He left space for her to respond and think—sometimes they even ended the conversation with a decision to revisit the topic after she had more time to reflect or investigate. Surprisingly, he found that his proposed solutions were more readily adopted.

The people who had the most insight into their problems were themselves! Using more of their own understanding and Kabir's brainstorming help, they could craft better solutions for their issues. Kabir expanded this process with others over the next month, and in no time, he had more energy and positive thinking.

PUTTING THE CONCEPT INTO PRACTICE

When we accept the world as it is, we deny our innate ability to see something better. By the same token, the better world we seek is within us, if only we can change our vision . . . At such times, we know what result we want to create, and we are moving toward it, even if we do not [yet] know how to get there.

—**ROBERT QUINN**, *Building the Bridge as You Walk On It*

What if you could make the exceptional moment the norm? Whether you face a challenge within yourself, with others, or on a work project, look around and identify what is still working. What is working well? What is working exceptionally well? What is making that possible? How might we create those same conditions elsewhere?

STEPS FOR APPRECIATIVE INQUIRY

- HONEST REVIEW
- LEVERAGE SKILLS
- ASK WHAT & WHY
- TAKE & GIVE SPACE
- ADVOCATE
- ACTION PLAN

Here are a few steps you can take to slow immediate self-advocacy and grow collaborative Appreciative Inquiry.

1. Rather than arriving with a solution that is fully baked or set in stone, arrive with an honest review of what you know / don't know and understand / don't understand. Leave space open for collaborative problem-solving. You might be surprised by what others saw that you might have missed or how they interpreted a complexity differently.

2. Continue to leverage your skills to find the root cause by investigating what's not working and why.

3. Don't stop there! Round out your investigation by asking what is working and why that might be.

4. Remember to take space and give space as you arrive collectively at a solution. Give others the freedom to share

the answer they come up with—you might even wait until everyone else has shared, especially if you are usually the first one to step onto the path.

5. Now is the time to advocate—when you have taken a collaborative approach, have seen the problem from multiple angles, and are ready to move forward with a team-based action plan.

Blending advocacy and inquiry helps us develop a strengths-based approach to expanding our internal self-awareness and external self-awareness, doing our jobs better, and helping us stay in a positive mindset towards work and others.

REFLECTION QUESTIONS

- How often do you find that your go-to response to problems is to immediately advocate for a solution?

- Why is positive thinking important to you? Why is "what's not working" thinking important to you?

- How might inquiry (staying curious) benefit the situation?

- What might be the dangers of being the one who knows everything or solves everything? To others? To yourself?

- What do you like about the concept of Appreciative Inquiry?

- What do you believe is the best approach to arriving at the best solution, given a problem? How has that shifted since learning about Appreciative Inquiry?

FURTHER READING AND REFERENCES

On the more casual side . . . books and resources to check out:

Kelm, Jacqueline Bascobert. (2005). *Appreciative Living.*

Quinn, Robert. (2004). *Building the Bridge as You Walk On It.*

On the more academic side . . . references we used:

Argyris, C. (1982). *Reasoning, Learning and Action: Individual and Organizational.*

Cooperrider, David. (1995). *Introduction to Appreciative Inquiry.*

Bulsuk, Karn. (2009). "An Introduction to 5-why." Bulsuk.com.

Toyoda, Sakichi. *Five Whys or Fishbone Technique*—Originally developed in the 1930s by Sakichi Toyoda, the founder of the Toyota Motor Corporation.

Watkins, Jane Magruder, Bernard Mohr, and Ralph Kelly. (2011). *Appreciative Inquiry: Change at the Speed of Imagination.*

1.5

MAKING DECISIONS AND TAKING ACTION | HEURISTICS AND PERSPECTIVE-TAKING

We can be blind to the obvious, and we are also blind to our blindness.

—DANIEL KAHNEMAN, *Thinking, Fast and Slow*

THE PROBLEM These are just *some* of the challenges you might encounter when making decisions and taking action where mitigating heuristics through perspective-taking can help.	• Do you make decisions without thinking? • Do you sound so sure of your decisions that there's no room for mistakes or additional information to be included? • Do you tend to focus on and take pride in being right and having the most logical way of thinking in the room? • Do you look back after making a decision and see apparent gaps in your logic? • Do you find it difficult to admit that there could be gaps in your logic?

Have you ever made a decision or judgment really quickly? So fast that you don't really know what thought went into the decision? In the previous topics, we've talked about reactions and how they are often based on emotions and subconscious remnants from our identities and past experiences. We've talked about how self-awareness, mindfulness, and strengths-based appreciative thinking can help slow down your reactions and provide time to craft a more thoughtful response.

For this topic, we turn our attention to action—not only the things we think or say but also the things we do. Our brains are wired to think fast and think slow, depending on the context. In some situations, when we think fast, we contribute effectively. Maybe we have a lot of expertise we can rely on to make a quick decision based on our intuition, but most often we aren't so lucky. We might not have all the information and knowledge we need but feel pressured by timelines or one of the Four Fatal Fears to appear decisive. What goes into the process of making a judgment call or decision? What influences our thinking outside of the feelings we have discussed so far? How can we maximize our effectiveness?

To answer these questions, we turn our attention from the leaps we make on the feeling side to the leaps we make on the neurological side and explore the neuroscience of heuristics.

MAKING DECISIONS AND TAKING ACTION THROUGH HEURISTICS AND PERSPECTIVE-TAKING

Psychosocial experts classify decisions we make as either rational, following bounded rationality, or nonrational.[16] In an ideal world, all of our decisions would be 100 percent rational, based on perfect facts and our assessment of those facts. However, our brains are highly efficient because the brain has created mental shortcuts to help us process and recall the information we have gathered over our lifetime of experience.

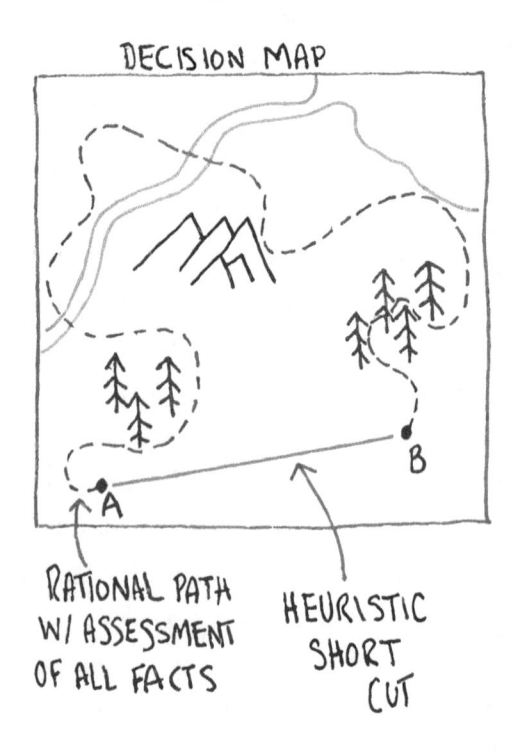

DECISION MAP — RATIONAL PATH W/ ASSESSMENT OF ALL FACTS / HEURISTIC SHORT CUT

These mental shortcuts are called *heuristics* and are considered a deviation from rational decision-making into bounded rationality.[17] In fixed rationality decision-making theory, we recognize that humans likely do not have all the information, analytical skills, or unlimited time needed to make a purely rational decision. Heuristics help relieve cognitive overload to make decisions quickly and efficiently. As Daniel Kahneman shares in his book *Thinking, Fast and Slow*:

> A general "law of least effort" applies to cognitive as well as physical exertion. The law asserts that if there are several ways of achieving the same goal, people will eventually gravitate to the least demanding course of action. Laziness is built deep into our nature.[18]

AVAILABILITY

All information → ● ← Recent information

REPRESENTATIVENESS

WOOF!

ANCHORING

$10 $5 | $10 | $15

Our brains use three main heuristics: availability, representativeness, and anchoring and adjustment.

- **AVAILABILITY:** How quickly information is available to us creates a sense of confidence in the accuracy of our decisions. The availability of information—how quickly it comes to mind—is one shortcut. We tend to think that things that happened recently are more likely to happen again.

- **REPRESENTATIVENESS:** We determine how closely related a person or an event is to a known category based on the number of perceived characteristics that person or event has with that category. The more characteristics, the more we believe a person or event fits into that category. For example, you might think that an individual who is outgoing, friends with everyone, and often shares his/her opinions at meetings might be a better leader than one who is more reserved and speaks only when it's important.

- **ANCHORING AND ADJUSTING:** When we have a starting belief (anchor), we often adjust new data and our thinking in relation to the anchor. The first piece of information is more heavily weighted, and then we tend to act based on the combination of the first information and subsequent information, rather than treating subsequent information as new and standalone. If our anchors are misguided, our adjustments and new information processing will be also.

While these heuristics are not inherently right or wrong, they influence how we think. This affects our perceptions of a situation and, ultimately, the actions we decide to take.

Overreliance on heuristics can cause the development of irrational biases. Whereas heuristics are usually based on tried-and-true rules of thumb drawn from the experiences of many individuals, cognitive biases become a rule of thumb or belief based on one person's often limited experience or exposure to social (rather than accurate) norms. More than one hundred cognitive biases have been identified.

When we make decisions, we need to be aware of heuristics, especially the cognitive biases that underlie our perception. Perspective-taking is a technique that helps mitigate the effects of heuristics. In the "Putting the Concept into Practice" section, we share more about considering additional perspectives before making decisions.

A STEM METAPHOR TO DRIVE THE POINT HOME: THE PATH OF LEAST RESISTANCE

In the sciences, the path of least resistance is a familiar concept. Nature takes shortcuts. For example, canyons are formed by water taking the path of least resistance and eroding solid rock.

Our minds work similarly. But the path of least resistance in our complex societal structure doesn't mean that it is necessarily the best path. In nature, the variables might be clear. But for human decisions, there is a lot we can't tabulate. That's why we want to be aware of our shortcuts and others' shortcuts and ensure we consider as complete a picture as we can before choosing a path.

A STORY IN ACTION

Samantha and Jered were peers at work. They were both subject matter experts in their field but had different career and college paths. Because of the nature of their jobs, they often had to collaborate on projects, but both were highly competitive.

Samantha had attended an elite science program at a university that ranked higher than Jered's. When making suggestions on what to do on a project, she often name dropped some of the professors she had worked with who were still thought leaders in the industry. On the other hand, Jered's school was very practical, and he came to the job with a lot of theoretical and practical knowledge.

When Jered brought suggestions to Samantha, she would quickly cut him off, making him think his perspective wasn't critical. Jered often thought to himself that he couldn't work with her anymore because she was not open to any of his ideas. After stewing over the way Samantha tended to talk to him, he started questioning why he was spending time thinking about her when there were so many other great things to think about.

Jered started reflecting on his perceptions of Samantha and wondered why she was cutting him off all the time. Instead of just wondering about it, he started asking her questions to see whether he could learn what she was trying to accomplish from her perspective. After asking questions, learning about Samantha, and seeing things from her point of view, he realized she was brilliant and had an excellent education. But he also realized he had a point, too. Her experiences on projects during college and in her professional career were more theoretical than practical.

Jered realized he needed Samantha to hear his perspective. Even though he was offering practical solutions, Samantha wasn't ready to hear him yet. She wanted to figure out the answers for herself, not just hear the explanation from Jered. After Jered realized this about Samantha, he was able to reframe the goals of their conversations. He perceived their conversations as being made up of two parts—the academic insight and the practical solutions. He would ask Samantha what she thought from a theory-based perspective and actively listen without interrupting. Then, he would share his view, analyzing the situation from a practical lens. Then together, they would combine their perspectives to arrive at a solution. Taking this approach led to better solutions than either of them would arrive at individually. The perspective-taking helped them be more collaborative and more successful.

PUTTING THE CONCEPT INTO PRACTICE

The confidence that individuals have in their beliefs depends mostly on the quality of the story they can tell about what they see, even if they see little.

—DANIEL KAHNEMAN, *Thinking, Fast and Slow*

Daniel Kahneman is an expert on heuristics, and in this quote, he implies that everything we think we understand is a story, made up of the facts we believe we see. Though we might have high confidence in the stories we tell ourselves, we might not be seeing reality accurately.

One way to understand how we think and to expand our perception of a given situation or interaction is to practice perspective-taking. Perspective-taking builds on and combines many of the capabilities we've already covered in this part.

Essentially, perspective-taking is the act of perceiving an event, interaction, or situation from alternative points of view. The key to successful perspective-taking is to understand the emotions, intentions, and behaviors of others to gain insight into how they see things. Here are some steps to try when practicing perspective-taking.

1. Notice the environment in which you are trying to understand alternative perspectives. Is it cooperative or competitive? When engaging in perspective-taking in a situation where the goal is to cooperate, you have a higher chance of successfully

connecting with the person. If the situation or person is viewed as competitive or confrontational, more cognitive effort is needed to consider the alternative perspectives.

2. Engage in mindfulness to create space before leaping to judgments and decisions.

3. Think about your Johari Window and use Appreciative Inquiry to ask questions and stay curious so you can quickly understand each other's perceptions.

4. Make decisions when you feel you have gathered enough differing perspectives to help overcome any biases stemming from your own cognitive heuristics.

Whether the situation is cooperative or competitive/confrontational, perspective-taking helps us better understand the way others think and the way we think. It offers us the opportunity to evaluate our thought processes compared to others and provides insight into our decisions and actions.

REFLECTION QUESTIONS

- Do you generally believe that there is more than one way to view and approach a situation? Why or why not?

- When engaged in a situation, how open are you to alternative points of view?

- How often are you reflecting on your perception versus others' perceptions?

- What has helped you see another person's interpretation of a situation?

- How much time do you allow for decision-making? What decisions do you feel confident making quickly? What types of decisions do you think you should make more slowly?

FURTHER READING AND REFERENCES

On the more casual side . . . a book to check out:

Kahneman, Daniel. (2013). *Thinking, Fast and Slow*.

On the more academic side . . . references we used:

Nairne, J. S. (2003). *Psychology of the Adaptive Mind*.

Simon, H. A. (1993). "Decision Making: Rational, Nonrational, and Irrational." *Educational Administration Quarterly*. https://doi.org/10.1177/0013161x93029003009.

PART 2

$$N = x_1 + x_2$$

THE FIRST PRINCIPLES OF RELATIONSHIPS

Little by little, as we live and work with others, we learn to break out of the shell of selfishness and self-centeredness where we seek to be brilliant and to prove our goodness, wisdom, and power. We all have to discover that there are others like us who have gifts and needs; no one of us is the center of the world. We all have a part to play. We need one another.

—JEAN VANIER, *Becoming Human*

Up to this point, we have focused on the N of X, you. You've received tools to grow your self-awareness and to expand your Johari Window (including noticing your reactions and their connection to the Four Fatal Fears), practicing mindfulness, acknowledging and developing strengths through Appreciative Inquiry, and understanding how you make decisions.

Ever heard the phrase, "If you want to go fast, go alone, but if you want to go far, go together"? This part will expand our sphere of focus from only yourself to you in relation to another. Expanding our sphere of focus is important since everything we do in life requires us to engage with at least one other human being (and sometimes a bot!). Being social is an essential human characteristic, and working and making a difference at scale can only happen through working with others.

In geometry, a vertex is a point at the intersection where two linear constructions meet. This meeting place is where we will start on our journey of forging healthy relationships. Eventually, we will work our way up to working in teams, managing others, and leading organizations. But for now, we will cover the fundamentals of relationships between yourself and one other using the following building blocks:

- **ACTING WITH THE NATURE OF RELATIONSHIPS IN MIND (PAGE 61):** You will be introduced to and empowered by the idea that relationships are co-created and dynamic.

- **PAUSING WHEN TRIGGERED (PAGE 73):** Interacting with others can often bring up a trigger, or negative presumption-based reactions. Using the Ladder of Inference as a visual mental model can help create a pause and more thoughtful action.

- **INVITING PEOPLE IN (PAGE 83):** You will learn the difference between a towards and away state and how to help create a Towards You state through the Four Agreements.

- **GROWING LONG-TERM BONDS (PAGE 94):** You will learn the different ongoing roles of taking, giving, and matching in relationships and the optimal ways to maintain and deepen relationships.

CONNECT BACK TO WHY

One of the sectors where STEM professionals are driving innovations is the energy sector. From nonprofits to traditional petroleum companies, from solar to nuclear power, the energy industry is undergoing tremendous transformation as sustainability concerns and geopolitical forces collide. Every day, professionals in these industries must use not only their technical talents but also their ability to judge and navigate the relationships in the room, in order to make a difference. Every person holds their own view of the present concerns and the future to come, and those views influence their decisions on what innovations and projects to support and what present operations to maintain. STEM professionals in these fields must be prepared to lead themselves and work through others effectively to create positive influence.

2.1

ACTING WITH THE NATURE OF RELATIONSHIPS IN MIND | THE CO-CREATION VIEW

Most accounts of human nature ignore our sociality altogether. Ask people what makes us special, and they will rattle off tried-and-true answers like "language," "reason," and "opposable thumbs." Yet the history of human sociality can be traced back at least as far as the first mammals more than 250 million years ago . . . These social adaptations are central to making us the most successful species on earth.

—MATTHEW LIEBERMAN, *Social*

THE PROBLEM	• Do you feel like there's nothing you can do to change someone's perception of you or yours of them?
These are just *some* of the challenges you might encounter that viewing relationships through a co-creation lens helps solve.	• Do you feel like you will always get the same outcome no matter what you try with someone?
	• Do you often feel like others are the problem?
	• Do you find yourself taking things personally or worrying excessively about what others think of you?
	• Do you tend to assume others are just like you?

We often think a relationship is all about us. Even though it's clear that there are two players in the game, we are inclined to view everything through the lens of "me" and "I." That can lead to several different problems.

Sometimes we assume the other person has the exact same wants, needs, issues, and beliefs as us. We project ourselves onto others. We don't leave space to learn about who they are. We might say to ourselves "I would feel this way, so they probably do, too," or "This feels important to me, and it should feel equally important to others."

Other times, we assume their every action has something to do with us, how they feel about us. We overanalyze, assume their intentions, and sabotage relationships. We might think "They excluded me from that meeting because they have a problem with me," or "They don't think my emails are important enough to reply to promptly."

We can also go the opposite direction—we believe that the other person is acting entirely on their own and that they are the problem. We might have had a single or a few experiences that caused us to form a judgment of that person that stays with us, no matter if they change or display different behavior at a later time. For example, a person shows up late to a meeting, and you start to think "They will show up late no matter what I do."

In each of these instances, our desire and motivation to collaborate decrease and unhealthiness in the relationship grows. However, none of these views of relationships are accurate or help set up a pair for success. That's because many issues center on a static concept of relationships—we think that those relationships are unchanging and independent of circumstances. To alter our view of the relationship and be more effective, we need to understand the fundamental nature of relationships: that they are co-created.

ACTING WITH THE NATURE OF RELATIONSHIPS IN MIND BY USING A CO-CREATION VIEW

Even though we would like relationships to be simple, they aren't as easy as one plus one equals two. Relationships are not predictable or formulaic. A simple mental model of relating to another person at work is often assumed to look like this: Person A and person B come together, each with a plan or agenda, and each completes that agenda in their time together. We often think of relationships as a simple exchange of ideas and actions. So, when you work with someone, your innate expectation might be that all you need is a plan, and your plan will be accomplished.

Even though relationships are part of our everyday experiences, they are also complex. A more useful mental model to keep in mind is that relationships are *co-created*. Two individuals who start interacting create something new between them. That something is a relationship. And each relationship will be different, depending on the people engaged in the interaction.

To be co-created means that the reality of a relationship does not simply exist as a static, predictable structure, nor is it created by one or the other person independently. It is created as the two people engage together continuously. In social psychology, this is formally called having a social constructionist view of relationships.

This is a dynamic view of relationships, which means that how you relate to someone can change. Picture a relationship like an unchoreographed dance between a couple—you're not the only one making a step; the other person makes a step in response, watching you and using their own ideas. Slowly but surely, a dance unfolds. At any moment, the dance could deviate from what you think might happen next. You might make an unexpected move. They might not like where things are headed and add something new to the mix.

In the book *Changing Conversations in Organizations*, Patricia Shaw puts forth this premise:

> We currently take it [conversation] for granted as a background to more important activities, as though conversation is carrying or transmitting the things we should be focusing our attention on. [Rather], I will describe and illustrate conversation as a process which has the intrinsic capacity to pattern itself. No single individual or group has control over the forms that emerge, yet between us we are continuously shaping and being shaped by those forms from within the flow of our responsive relating.[1]

SAM

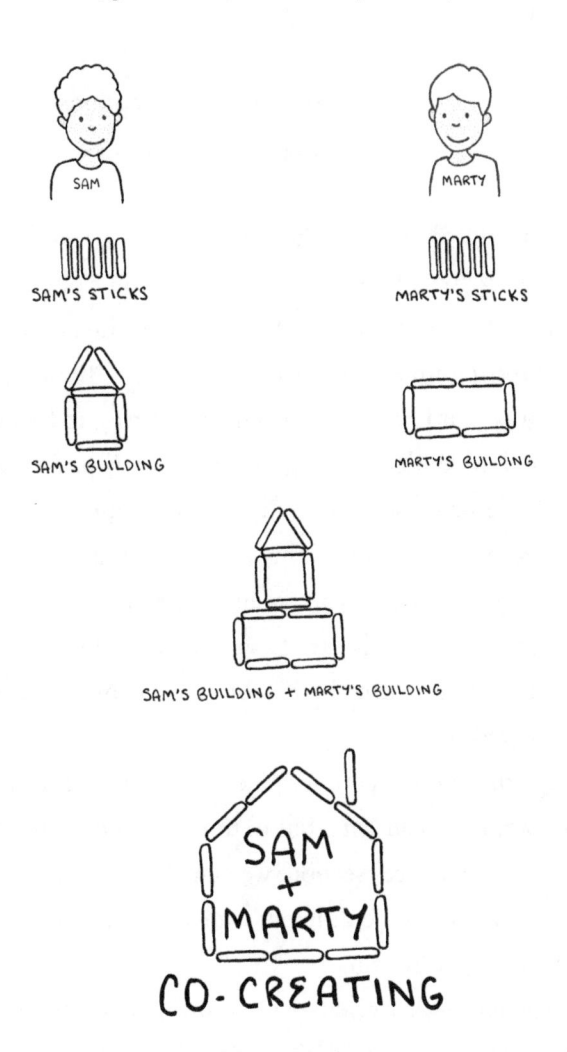

MARTY

SAM'S STICKS

MARTY'S STICKS

SAM'S BUILDING

MARTY'S BUILDING

SAM'S BUILDING + MARTY'S BUILDING

SAM
+
MARTY

CO-CREATING

She goes on further to describe the transformative activity of conversing as follows:

> When we converse, we are not decoding words and sentences as signs which represent some object to which we are referring, nor are we simply interpreting bodily signals from others as a "mental" activity. Rather we are immersed in a sensuous flow of patterned feeling, a kind of ethos in which words have the

power to move or to arrest us, shift our perceptions and actions because we are communicating as intelligent bodies.[2]

Once you understand that how you relate to another is a constantly emerging dynamic—not only reliant on you, your identity, your plan, and your reactions but also reliant on theirs—you are ready to engage in setting up a relationship for success. The first thing that becomes clear is that knowing yourself and getting to know the other is fundamental to understanding the relationship. As Dr. Miriam Lacey (PhD and professor) often says to her students (one of whom was Crystal Kadakia, author of this book) of organizational change, "You want to get to know your issues, their issues, and the issues you're creating together." In part 1, we established the tools to know ourselves better; if you use these tools and techniques, part of the equation is solved for you.

Knowing the other part of the equation—knowing another person—is complex because it requires time and energy. In the "Putting the Concept into Practice" section, we start breaking down this complexity by introducing three different categories of relationships based on the work of Edgar Schein.

Most of what we learn about relationships is done in real time. Relationships emerge; they aren't predestined to be a certain way or end at a specific outcome. This can be scary because you don't know where you will go together, but reacting out of fear leads to unhealthy dynamics, such as control, exclusion, dominance, and more. Instead, consider the co-creative mental model as an exciting idea, one that holds surprises, possibilities, and opportunities to go further than you could imagine (or control) alone. You'll find yourself leading with openness, compassion, respect, and innovation and drawing others towards you.

PUTTING THE CONCEPT INTO PRACTICE

The culture of Do and Tell does not teach us how to change pace, decelerate, take stock of what we are doing, observe ourselves and others, try new behaviors, build new relationships.

—EDGAR H. SCHEIN, *Humble Inquiry*

When is it the right time and context to intentionally apply the co-creation view of relationships? We say intentionally because, of course, co-creation is happening whether you try or not! But there are certain relationships you could consider seriously investing your time and energy in to understand the co-creative dynamic at work—that is, going beyond just having a conversation with another person.

Think of it this way: There's paying attention to what you want to say, paying attention to what the other person is saying, and stepping back from both of those to pay attention to what the conversation is saying. When should you actively step back and assess the conversation itself? Edgar Schein outlined three different categories of relationships:[3]

1. **TASK-BASED OR TRANSACTIONAL RELATIONSHIPS:** For a task, the interaction with another person is transactional. This could mean an exchange of goods or services or an exchange of communication, like ordering coffee from Starbucks, supplies from Amazon, or getting flipped off on the freeway. This interaction is episodic and may or may not happen again soon. If you have limited capacity, mentally diving into the co-creative dynamic here is unlikely to be helpful.

2. **PROCESS-BASED OR PERSONAL RELATIONSHIPS:** The process is when we enter a deeper connection with another person in forming joint

ideas or goals. These collaborative ideas or goals could include working with a vendor on the supply chain or a team for product development. The interaction becomes more personalized because you inquire about others and reveal your own thoughts. This type of sharing is normal and necessary to move forward. You seek to see the other person's point of view and for them to see yours. There is a high probability that you will see and engage with this person regularly. Making space to get to know the other person and inquiring often about their intent is crucial. Having a co-creation mental model can be very helpful in making these relationships effective and efficient. You will want to watch out for your triggers and create a Towards You state (which are covered in the next two topics in this part).

3. **TRANSFORMATIVE OR INTIMATE RELATIONSHIPS:** The last category is transformative relationships, in which the intent is to *transform* the interaction into a relationship with a deep level of intimacy. Typically, these are people we interact with weekly or daily. And since the relationships tend to be longer-term, persistence in getting to know the other person is key. Having a co-creative view is essential for these relationships. This view is particularly helpful when you feel stuck and may help you notice when you are holding on to static ideas about the other person that may no longer be true. In addition to the other topics in this part, the topic "Growing Long-Term Bonds" may be especially helpful.

These categories show up in the workplace all the time. Knowing these three types of relationships creates a framework for choosing the level of relationship we want to have with another person.

1. First, determine what the intent of the relationship is. Is it task-oriented (one and done), process-oriented (ongoing, where trust is needed), or transformative (ongoing, and trust is essential)?

2. Second, determine what kind of relationship you want with this person after your first conversation.

3. Third, determine the level of time and energy you will commit and the questions you will ask to understand what you are co-creating together.

A STEM METAPHOR TO DRIVE THE POINT HOME: NEWTON'S THIRD LAW OF MOTION

Let's look at Newton's Third Law of Motion—for every action, there is an equal and opposite reaction. Two objects move, but it is only together that a combined movement pattern is created. A variety of natural forces can act on objects or can be applied between objects, such as gravitational, electrical, or magnetic forces.

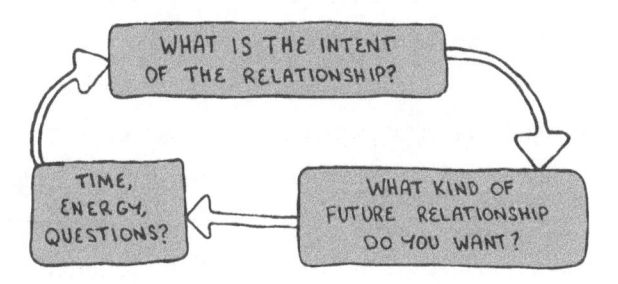

People are similar—there could be many forces at work that you don't see that create a reaction (think back to part 1 and how other people have their own Johari Window). The same becomes exponentially true for you and working with others. Together, you create a movement pattern.

A STORY IN ACTION

Sasha is a busy person. He shows up early for work and stays late. He's not one to socialize with others and often keeps to himself at work. His job is very task-oriented and requires little dependence on others to complete his part of the work. His company recently conducted a reorganization that created a new colleague, Enrique, with whom Sasha will need to collaborate daily.

In the first three weeks of the new reorganization, Enrique would reach out to Sasha every morning to check in and get to know Sasha. Sasha would take the time to answer Enrique's calls, but the conversation was transactional. After the fourth week of putting forth the effort with little reciprocation from Sasha, Enrique stopped calling him to check in. A week went by, and Sasha thought it was unusual that Enrique stopped checking in but assumed it was Enrique's issue, not his.

Later that week, Sasha ran into Lara at the town hall meeting. She was a colleague Enrique had worked with at a different company. Lara shared her excitement that Sasha was working with Enrique since they had so much in common. Sasha was surprised and wondered what made her say that. He went on LinkedIn and found that they had attended the same college and had several parallel connections and interests.

Sasha reflected on his interactions with Enrique. He realized he had treated his relationship with Enrique as a transactional one. Furthermore, he realized that the drop-off in communication was not Enrique's problem; it was his own. Sasha realized that he enjoyed talking with Enrique and checking in with him and that his actions had caused Enrique to withdraw. Sasha reached out to Enrique to begin building a more transformative relationship.

REFLECTION QUESTIONS

- What do you think about the concept of a relationship as a co-created entity?

- What negative consequences might you experience with a simple transactional view of relationships?

- What benefits might you experience with a more complex, co-created view?

- Can you think of a time when you found value in an organic, unplanned conversation?

- Can you think of a time when you were hoping for a particular outcome with someone, but things just didn't go as you hoped?

- Can you think of a time when you had a plan but were open to where the conversation would go, and you were happy with the outcome?

- Thinking about the three kinds of relationships discussed in this topic, what kind of interactions do you typically have?

FURTHER READING AND REFERENCES

On the more casual side . . . books and resources to check out:

Lieberman, Matthew. (2013). *Social: How Our Brains Are Wired to Connect.*

Schein, E. (2013). *Humble Inquiry: The Gentle Art of Asking Instead of Telling.*

On the more academic side . . . references we used:

Jehn, K. A., and C. Bendersky. (2003). "Intragroup Conflict in Organizations: A Contingency Perspective on the Conflict-Outcome Relationship." *Research in Organizational Behavior.* https:/doi.org/10.1016/S0191-3085(03)25005-X.

Shaw, Patricia. (2002). *Changing Conversations in Organizations: A Complexity Approach to Change.*

2.2

PAUSING WHEN TRIGGERED | THE LADDER OF INFERENCE

Nothing in this world is good or bad, but thinking makes it so.

—**WILLIAM SHAKESPEARE,** *Hamlet*

THE PROBLEM These are just *some* of the challenges you might encounter that pausing when triggered helps solve.	• Do you jump to conclusions, especially about people... and find out later your conclusions weren't quite right? • Have you ever reacted, said, or done something out of anger, hurt, or other negative feelings that you later regret? • Have you ever found yourself acting in passive-aggressive ways—which are quiet ways of undermining a person or situation due to negative conclusions you've drawn?

Have you ever been in a meeting and felt frustrated, annoyed, or angry by a person in the room? Worst yet, imagine your boss assigns you to work with a person you have a heavy resistance towards working with. When you think about this person, your brain uses your feelings about them to generate beliefs about them that often go untested. You assume your beliefs about this person are true, and real data seems to support this truth. But sometimes, our overreaction to a situation or a person triggers our emotions, and they can overshadow our cognition.

For example, Hailey is a fellow colleague who always shows up when the work is done. She doesn't openly ask for credit, but she, along with everyone else, gets credit for the work. This has happened a few times. Now, when she receives credit for the team's work (unjustifiably, in your point of view), it triggers you. When she talks about the team's work, you feel a spike of anger that prevents you from hearing what she says. The triggers influence your thought process, and your brain leaps ahead and makes abstract judgments about her. These judgments affect your tone when you talk to her. You know anger isn't the best place to work from, but you can't seem to get out of it.

Being triggered happens every day. We can explain and overcome these leaps to adverse judgments and actions through a self-leadership concept called the Ladder of Inference.[4]

PAUSING WHEN TRIGGERED USING THE LADDER OF INFERENCE

I have become more aware of (1) how true emotions can feel during crucial moments, and (2) how false they really are.
—**KERRY PATTERSON AND COLLEAGUES,** *Crucial Conversations*

The Ladder of Inference is a mental model, developed by Chris Argyris, that shows how we leap from data in our environment to misguided assumptions, conclusions, or beliefs. In general, the model shares that we jump to assumptions, especially those that confirm our previous understanding, without testing or acknowledging new data, when we hear or observe something.

In part 1, we described the many possible sources of misguided conclusions, including the Blind area in our Johari Window, our emotions when triggered by the Four Fatal Fears, and the neurological shortcuts, or heuristics, we tend to make to deal with complexity. By now, hopefully, you have been convinced that questioning what you think is a worthwhile endeavor! The Ladder of Inference visual helps you slow down and question, so you can make a shift towards inquiry and response rather than reaction. Here is an explanation of each level of the ladder and how you migrate from one step to the next.

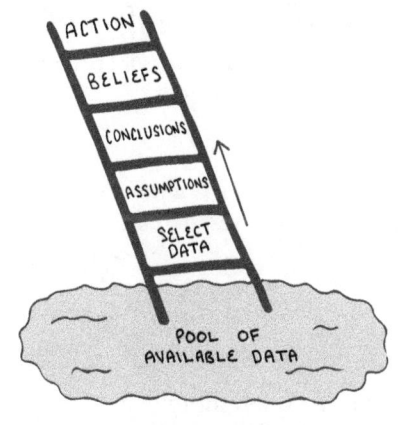

RAPID LEAPS HAPPEN IN SECONDS

- **POOL OF AVAILABLE DATA:** At the base of the ladder, you observe someone's behavior. Their behavior is data for you to use. The data you collect is the starting point, where you begin to interpret what their behavior really means to you.

- **SELECT DATA:** You pick out various bits of data based on what fits your mental model (your internal representation of the situation) or your thought process.

- **ASSUMPTIONS:** The next step on the ladder is the leap of abstraction in which you interpret what you experienced. It's an assumption of intention and understanding. The meaning you attach to the observed behavior could be correct or could be wildly misguided.

- **CONCLUSIONS:** Although your assumptions are misguided and are definitely untested, your misguided thoughts lead to misguided conclusions that quickly propel you to the next stage.

- **BELIEFS:** At this point, your conclusions feel irrefutable. It becomes an uphill battle to convince yourself otherwise, and all subsequent data points continue to reinforce these beliefs.

- **ACTION:** Now, you are at the top of the ladder. You have no choice but to act based on your deeply misguided thought process.

Climbing the ladder could literally take only seconds. And the next time you observe this person again, you will look for data that continues to confirm your experience of them. You tend to look for data that strengthens your assumptions about the person rather than approaching the interaction with an open mind.

To make the transition from simply leading ourselves to working with and leading others, it is vital that—in the moment when you are triggered—you understand why you are triggered and come back down the ladder to restart the process of interpreting and understanding your interactions with others. In the "Putting the Concept into Practice" section, we explain how to use some of the skills from part 1 to pause when triggered and create the opportunity to have a more open dialogue.

PUTTING THE CONCEPT INTO PRACTICE

Patterson and colleagues put it bluntly in their book *Crucial Conversations*: "When people purposefully withhold meaning from one another, individually smart people can do collectively stupid things."[5] Slow yourself down on the Ladder of Inference by practicing some of the skills we've already shared.

The goal is to stop yourself before you climb too far and too fast up the Ladder of Inference. You want to transition out of a habit of making snap judgments and conclusions and into a practice of having productive conversations that help you test your assumptions.

- **MINDFULNESS:** Slowing down, stepping back, and mapping your thoughts are all great ways to create the pause. It's okay to say you need time to process—and this is far better than racing up the ladder and having to mitigate consequences later. As hard as it can be to slow down, take a deep breath, make space for yourself, and allow your reactions to emerge when you are by yourself.

- **TAKE A CO-CREATED VIEW:** Rather than holding on to a static, rigid view that this person is the way they are, you know how they are, and they will not change, adopt a dynamic perspective. You can change what happens next—and so can they. What is the goal you have in mind for this relationship? Is that intent positive or negative? Your goal might be to share information (collaboration), show gratitude (appreciation), or share where ideas or values are not aligned (functional conflict). Knowing that we co-create the relationships we are in, considering our intent helps us process information about the relationship and move towards the relationship we want during and after the conversation.

- **HEURISTICS AND PERSPECTIVE-TAKING:** We are good at *judging*—applying our interpretation to—someone's behaviors, but we are terrible at interpreting observable behaviors for what they really are: simply actions. The meaning behind the action is often unknown to the observer. Assess what mental shortcuts you might be making—are you looking to confirm what you think you know rather than keeping an open mind? Are you comparing situations that really aren't analogous at all?

- **LOOK OUT FOR THE FOUR FATAL FEARS:** Are you triggered? By what, exactly? Are you trying to compensate for a fear you have by jumping to conclusions?

- **JOHARI WINDOW:** What don't you know? And what don't you know that you don't know? Start thinking of curious questions. Being self-aware will open up the window of opportunity and help you better relate to and understand the other's perspective.

- **APPRECIATIVE INQUIRY:** Ask questions and then listen to understand—by listening, we can be mindful of what the person is saying. Former US Secretary of State Dean Rusk famously said, "One of the best ways to persuade others is with your ears—by listening to them." Ask questions for clarification, get to the root cause of the misalignment, see what's working well, and ask for confirmation (or clarification) of your understanding. Reflect on what you're hearing. In English, words have multiple meanings and are often used out of context. Discovering what they mean will help determine the signal (what they mean) from the noise (lots of words). "Did you mean x when you said y?" and "I'm sorry, I didn't understand what you meant just then" are ways you can explore what the other person is trying to communicate to you.

Later, in part 3, we will take this step—pausing when triggered—to the next level by sharing the Crucial Conversations approach to managing conflict. For now, bringing together the different techniques we've discussed so far is a significant step on the journey.

A STEM METAPHOR TO DRIVE THE POINT HOME: REVERSIBLE VS. IRREVERSIBLE PROCESSES

In thermodynamics, two paths of a process transform system are reversible and irreversible.[6] The reversible process is the path that can reverse to return the system to its original state without changing the properties of the system. The irreversible process is more complicated and cannot simply be reversed; it inadvertently changes the properties of a system.

These two paths are like our choice to pause before reacting to triggers or not. By taking a pause, we have the chance to reverse the ascent up the Ladder of Inference and test our assumptions, judgments, and misguided beliefs we have generated. Since we deal with it using our internal and external self-awareness, we can self-correct, and the relationship is preserved.

However, suppose we decide not to have a productive conversation and go ahead and ascend the Ladder of Inference. In that case, we might be misguided in our thoughts about the other person and journey down an irreversible process. Because we get stuck in a reflective loop, we can see nothing good about this person. Our actions towards that person could strain the relationship, making the changes irreversible and impossible to repair or, even worse, making it impossible to develop any level of trust.

A STORY IN ACTION

After the team meeting, Martin, a colleague, approached Savita and said, "Our boss, Farbod, doesn't care about people."

Savita blew off the comment but later started thinking about her observations of Farbod's behaviors. She recalled that he is brief in his conversations with others. Sometimes he interrupts others while they are speaking. He seldom gives praise in private or public forums. In fact, he had attended none of the virtual happy hours during the pandemic.

She concluded to herself, "Martin is right; Farbod doesn't care about people."

One time Farbod had remembered her birthday, but that was just the one time. And the other day, Ishmael echoed Martin's comments about Farbod's lack of care and interest. Savita started climbing up the Ladder of Inference. What had been a passing comment had turned into data, or a "fact," proving that Farbod doesn't care about people.

In her one-on-one communication with Farbod, her leap from selected data to belief influenced how she showed up to the meeting.

She was very short and to the point with Farbod. He asked if she was doing okay, and she responded, "I'm fine."

After reading her behavior, Farbod cut the meeting short, thinking she must be busy. He decided to give her back some time in her day. Because of the shorter meeting, Savita walked out of Farbod's office having confirmed her opinion about Farbod with more "evidence" that Martin and Ishmael were right. Farbod doesn't care about people.

REFLECTION QUESTIONS

- Can you recall a time when you were triggered? Have you ever climbed the Ladder of Inference? Can you remember the impact that it had on you and your behavior towards that person?

- Do you think it's helpful to climb the Ladder of Inference? Why or why not?

- Think about your most challenging relationships. What do you think the benefits of staying off the Ladder of Inference could be?

- What can you do to pause when you are triggered?

- How can you prevent from ascending the Ladder of Inference?

- What is one thing you will try the next time you notice you have started climbing the Ladder of Inference?

FURTHER READING AND REFERENCES

On the more casual side . . . a book to check out:

Patterson, K., J. Grenny, R. McMillan, and A. Switzler. (2012). *Crucial Conversations: Tools for Talking When the Stakes Are High.*

On the more academic side . . . references we used:

Argyris, Chris, and Donald A. Schön. (1978). *Organizational Learning: A Theory of Action Perspective.*

Ling, Samuel J., William Moebs, and Jeff Sanny. (2016). *University Physics, Volume 2.*

2.3

INVITING PEOPLE IN | A "TOWARDS YOU" STATE

Here's the problem. Most people are thinking about what they don't want, and they're wondering why it shows up over and over again.

—**RHONDA BYRNE,** *The Secret*

THE PROBLEM These are just *some* of the challenges you might encounter that inviting people in helps solve.	<ul><li>Do you want to attract people to work with you?</li><li>Do you want positive collaborations where you and others feel liked, valued, or otherwise appreciated?</li><li>Do you feel like you can threaten or otherwise scare others away?</li><li>Do you wonder why others don't actively reach out to you?</li><li>Do you believe you work better alone but find this hurting your career?</li></ul>

Many of us grew up without intentionally learning how to improve our interpersonal skills. Depending on the culture you identify with, and the family culture you were born into, how we form relationships and deal with differences vary widely. Therefore, much of the interpersonal skills we bring to the workforce is based on a lifetime of trial and error. And, depending on how well our past life experiences match the environment we are in now, we can be more or less successful in inviting and attracting positive relationships.

Sometimes things work out, but in other cases, they don't. When all we have is the trial-and-error approach, it's unclear specifically what worked well or how to replicate it since every person and situation is unique. Especially if we have changed geographies, our old cultural norms may not still hold true. Often, when faced with challenges, we approach them in the wrong way and react in a way that drives the other person away or puts them on the defensive. Not because we want things to get worse but because we might not know the right moves to make it better. As we learned in the last topic, when someone is resistant towards you, it's easy to make assumptions about their resistance and climb up the Ladder of Inference.

Rather than reacting based on past patterns, having a clear set of principles that you can consistently rely on will help you create a "towards state," rather than an "away state." This topic will discuss the concept of a Towards You state from a neurological perspective and introduce the Four Agreements to create a Towards You state from a relational perspective.

INVITING OTHERS IN BY CREATING A "TOWARDS YOU" STATE

Our sociality is woven into a series of bets that evolution has laid down again and again throughout mammalian history. These bets come in the form of adaptations that are selected because they promote survival and reproduction. These adaptations intensify the bonds we feel with those around us and increase our capacity to predict what is going on in the minds of others so that we can better coordinate and cooperate with them. The pain of social loss and the ways that an audience's laughter can influence us are no accidents. To the extent that we can characterize evolution as designing our modern brains, this is what our brains were wired for: reaching out to and interacting with others.

—MATTHEW LIEBERMAN, *Social*

You might think that there's nothing you can do about your social capability or that trying to change how you interact with others will be inauthentic. After all, you've been who you are your whole life, right? But just like any other part of our lives, there's actually a lot we can do to become better citizens of our communities while still being true to ourselves. As highlighted in the quote above from the work of researcher Matthew Lieberman, the brain evolved to connect with other people. Whole regions of our neurology are dedicated to specific social capabilities that empower connection. In other words, we have built-in strengths towards inviting people in.

Neuroscientist David Rock explains how our brains feel rewarded through a "towards state." A towards state is when a person feels safe, comfortable, and even excited. The concept of a Towards You state was coined by David Rock in his seminal book *Your Brain at Work*. As he shares:

> The limbic system [a neural region of the brain] is constantly making *toward* or *away* decisions. Emotions such as curiosity, happiness, and contentment are toward responses. Anxiety, sadness, and fear, on the other hand, are away responses . . . And we have a tendency to walk towards, but run away. The limbic system fires up far more intensely when it perceives a danger compared to when it senses a reward. Even the strongest toward emotion (lust) is unlikely to make you run, whereas fear can do so in an instant. The toward emotions are more subtle, more easily displaced, and harder to build on.[7]

As you can probably guess, the triggers that lead up the Ladder of Inference and the Four Fatal Fears create an away state for you personally. This can lead you to react in an ineffective, unhealthy manner. So how do you stop people from feeling that way about you? What can you do to minimize the chances of creating triggers in people around you that might be perceived as threatening by the brain? A statement ascribed to Werner Erhard, creator of the self-development program the Landmark Forum, captures this concept: "The reaction you got was the communication you intended." The idea is that when faced with a threat, humans fight, flee, or freeze, and these are all responses you want to avoid sparking within someone else.

In *Your Brain at Work*, David Rock outlines the five factors that create a towards state in our limbic systems. The acronym SCARF is an easy mnemonic to remember when you feel threatened or notice a person feeling threatened around you.

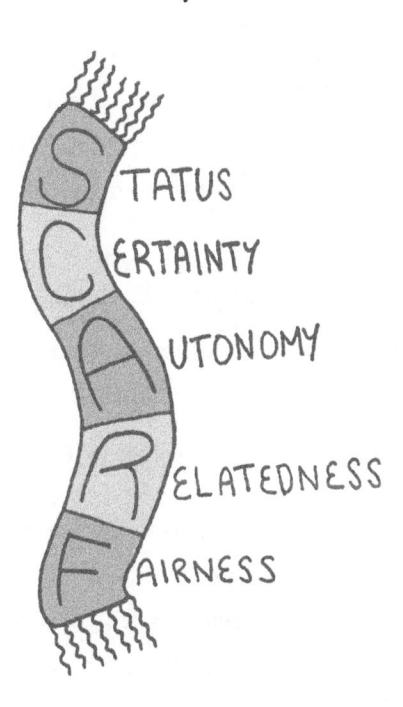

STATUS
CERTAINTY
AUTONOMY
RELATEDNESS
FAIRNESS

- **STATUS:** A person's sense of relative importance to others in a room. How is interpersonal status being elevated or diminished or held equivalent to others? If the person feels diminished, feelings of being threatened will likely follow.

- **CERTAINTY:** A person's sense that they know what's coming next and the amount of uncertainty in a situation. Highly uncertain conditions increase anxiety and panic and arouse an away state. Adding a little certainty, a slight sense of knowing—even if only perceived certainty versus real certainty—can reduce feelings of threat.

- **AUTONOMY:** A person's sense of control and perception of choice over an environment or situation. When given no choice (or perceiving that there is no choice), feelings of threat and stress prevail.

- **RELATEDNESS:** A person's sense that they are similar to others, enough to feel a bit of trust and empathy, increases the towards state and positive emotions. Differences still exist and are acknowledged, but the person can establish a sense of relatedness.

- **FAIRNESS:** A person's sense that they are being treated fairly is a significant factor in creating a towards state. Being mistreated creates hostility that easily escalates into an away state quickly.

You can use these five domains to help plan a meeting where you hope to create a towards state. You can also use these to assess what might be going on for you when you feel threatened. You can also notice whether someone feels threatened around you and evaluate which of the five domains might be playing a role. In the "Putting the

Concept into Practice" section, we go beyond assessing and into action by using the Four Agreements to create a Towards You state.

PUTTING THE CONCEPT INTO PRACTICE

The Four Agreements shared by Don Miguel Ruiz give you the power to maintain a Towards You state.[8] The Four Agreements are:

1. **BE IMPECCABLE WITH YOUR WORD:** Because we use words every day, they can be used like careless commodities. Yet, words are powerful and affect us all in various ways. Something you meant or intended but never said can never be assumed to be understood by others. Working together cannot get done without communication. Understanding this power helps us use our words to bring out the mutual goals of the interactions, our interpretations or points of view, and form a collaborative connection. These communications inherently convey your commitments. When something changes, communicating becomes even more important.

    As shared in David Rock's SCARF model, two of the domains that help our brains feel most comfortable are certainty and fairness. The greater the ambiguity, the more likely it is that anxiety and the fight or flight syndrome will be provoked. When someone betrays a commitment, the other can feel the sting of unfairness, creating an away rather than a towards reaction. Using your words and sticking to them with integrity creates greater certainty and fairness and is a powerful way to maintain a Towards You state.

2. **TAKE NOTHING PERSONALLY:** Although it might feel like it, not everything is about you. Sometimes, people step outside of

their bubble and see things from a higher vantage point. When they do, it usually doesn't feel like it's personal. Other times, people filter reality through their own needs, wants, and insecurities. Often what they say is based solely on their world. They might be projecting or critical about something important to them and may fail to take your view into account. Perhaps someone says something that you have thought of yourself. We are complex beings, with many things competing for our time and attention. Someone's actions towards you might have nothing to do with you; you are the person standing in front of them when they are not at their best.

In these situations, by not taking what they say personally, you avoid adverse reactions that might turn them away and instead create space to empathize with them and give them a choice.

David Rock shares that giving people a sense of autonomy in a situation and treating them like friends rather than foes can create a positive state. Empathizing with their underlying need can help grow the feeling that you can relate to each other. Letting them know that you might see things differently gives the impression that there is a choice in handling the situation—both for you and for them. Now, both of you feel empowered and together in a situation, rather than putting each other down.

3. **DON'T MAKE ASSUMPTIONS:** The things that can hurt you the most are the things we are not aware of. Whether you have internal self-awareness of how it is affecting you or external awareness of how it is affecting others, suspending judgment

gives us the brainpower to evaluate before acting. Jumping up the Ladder of Inference is the easiest way to create a negative reaction and drive a relationship away. Instead, giving people the same benefit of the doubt you would like them to give you and assuming the best intentions of someone (unless otherwise communicated) creates a towards state. David Rock says that the feeling of equal status creates a positive neurotransmitter action in the brain. When someone feels less than or judged, negative neural activity lends to an away state.

4. **ALWAYS DO YOUR BEST:** Doing our best and feeling good about the effort we put into any task is all we can ask of anyone. As we do our best work, we put ourselves in a position to do even better. And, when we aren't doing our best, we don't find it difficult to admit it. In doing so, we find we don't always have to be the best in the room—by always doing our best, we have positive relationships in our work groups that lift everyone up, using all of our strengths to achieve complex goals.

A STEM METAPHOR TO DRIVE THE POINT HOME: MOLECULAR BONDS

Molecules can bond together in many different ways—and often they do not bond at all. Sometimes, like in an ionic bond, the bond is more transactional. In others, like covalent bonds, they share more of one another. Other compounds are immiscible and can't mix. Thinking about how materials bond can be a metaphor for your nature and whether you are creating a towards state for others or an away, or unmixing, state.

A STORY IN ACTION

Marty had been with the company for some time. Samuel, her boss, offered her the opportunity to take on a special project that would give her significant experience and improve her visibility within the company, which might help her win a promotion. She would manage a team that was known for not liking outsiders. She knew she could do an outstanding job and wanted to withhold judgment about the team members. She was determined to treat them with respect and not prejudge them.

Before approaching the team for the first time, she spent time planning different scenarios of how the team might react to her and how she could use words to show what they could expect of her. After her initial meeting with the team, she faced heavy resistance. She was a little disappointed, given the time she had spent trying to make a positive impact. Since she and the team barely knew one another, she believed this was not personal and kept her words consistent with the impact she wanted to create. She continued to create certainty in her behavior and interactions with the team.

Although the team was resistant to outsiders, she realized some individuals connected with her one-on-one. These one-on-one interactions debunked her assumptions about the team and their resistance. She was able to relate to these individuals and maintain a sense of fairness. It was individuals, not the team, who were resistant to outsiders. She knew it was her choice how to react, and each team member also had that autonomy. Marty determined that nothing, including the resisters, would hinder her from doing her best.

It took several months, many repetitions of a consistent message, not taking things personally, not going after others personally, testing her assumptions, and doing her best. Marty finally forged a relationship with the resisters that benefitted the team and the project's output.

REFLECTION QUESTIONS

- What level of confidence do you have in creating a Towards You state? Why?

- What does a towards state relationship look like? Can you think of an example relationship you feel magnetically attracted to in your community?

- Is there a relationship you are concerned about turning into an away state? How might the Four Agreements help you create a sense of equal status, certainty, relatedness, fairness, and autonomy?

- How might deliberately practicing the Four Agreements, not just in times of conflict, benefit your relationships in the long term?

FURTHER READING AND REFERENCES

On the more casual side . . . books and resources to check out:

Byrne, Rhonda. (2006). *The Secret.*

Lieberman, Matthew. (2014). *Social: Why Our Brains Are Wired to Connect.*

Rock, David. (2020). *Your Brain at Work.*

Ruiz, Don Miguel. (2018). *The Four Agreements: A Practical Guide to Personal Freedom.*

2.4

GROWING LONG-TERM BONDS | GIVERS, MATCHERS, AND TAKERS

Be slow to fall into friendship; but when thou art in, continue firm and constant.

—SOCRATES

Being a giver is not good for a 100-yard dash, but it's valuable in a marathon.

—ADAM GRANT, *Give and Take*

THE PROBLEM These are just *some* of the challenges you might encounter that growing long-term bonds helps solve.	• Do you feel isolated and disconnected? • Do you feel like your relationships aren't high quality, deep, or reliable even though you spend a lot of time at work? • Do you struggle with staying in touch and forming longer-term bonds?

Relationships are investments that can be as volatile as the stock market. As much as we would like to set it and forget it, they require mutual energy, effort, and desire to succeed. When we engage in a relationship, we enter with the hope for a mutual benefit, known as reciprocity.

The rule of reciprocity is that if someone does something for us, we will try to repay in kind, whether it is an emotional give and take, physical act, or other act. When we believe in reciprocity, a person can give freely to another with the confidence that they will not lose anything—the exchange of giving and taking benefits the individual relationship and the community at large.

However, what happens when you can't count on reciprocity? Over the years, we have learned to watch out for people who take and do not give back. We expend great effort to prevent ourselves from being victims of their taking. This prompts us to enter relationships with caution. We hold back until we are sure there is a mutual benefit to the relationship. Especially in a digital age, where we often can't see one another, it's easy to become a victim of scams or be ghosted.

Ideally, instead of showing up with caution, we would consistently show up, intending to be the best version of ourselves, and do our best to strengthen the relationship by building a Towards You state. Regardless of your initial approach to relationships, when we find we have started a healthy relationship, we want to continue maintaining, adjusting, and growing that relationship as needed. To help keep our commitment, in this topic, we will explore three types of relationships, as defined by researcher Adam Grant.

GROWING LONG-TERM BONDS BY GIVING, TAKING, OR MATCHING

According to conventional wisdom, highly successful people have three things in common: motivation, ability, and opportunity. [But there is] a fourth ingredient, one that's critical but often neglected: success depends heavily on how we approach our interactions with other people. Every time we interact with another person at work, we have a choice to make: do we try to claim as much value as we can, or contribute value without worrying about what we receive in return?

—ADAM GRANT, *Give and Take*

Researcher Adam Grant studied givers and takers to understand relationships better and to understand who is more likely to succeed in the workplace. He also defined a third category of relationship, which he called *matchers*.

TAKER

GIVER

MATCHER

Let's take a closer look at takers, givers, and matchers.

- **TAKERS:** Takers clearly enter the relationship to see how much they can get out of it. They are willing to help others out as long as their benefit outweighs the cost. Takers are self-promoters who want to make sure they get credit. They play a zero-sum game to win while others lose. Their most significant concern is how to get more power. The question they consistently ask as they approach relationships is "What can you do for me?"

- **GIVERS:** Givers are big-picture thinkers. They enter into a relationship to grow the relationship so everyone gets more. They follow the logic that two is greater than one, also known as an abundance mentality. Their most significant concern is how they can help people the most. The question they consistently ask as they approach relationships is "What can I do for you?"

- **MATCHERS:** Matchers are concerned with an even exchange and give to others on a quid pro quo basis. They tend to seek out relationships to help them in their immediate circumstances. To protect themselves from being vulnerable to takers, matchers are skeptical of others and think of the work environment as a zero-sum game. They often keep a scorecard of favors given and received. The question they consistently ask as they approach relationships is "If I do this for you, will you do that for me?"

Grant gained a surprising insight from his research: Out of the three, givers were both the *least* and the *most* successful in the workplace in terms of performance and career growth. In contrast, both takers and matchers most often landed in the middle of the success ladder. Givers could be the least successful because the time and effort they spend helping others reduces the time they spend helping themselves. They can have the lowest productivity. Although he found that givers can be taken advantage of, if they create boundaries to preserve their time, they can become highly successful—far beyond takers and matchers. Here's what Grant found:

> Givers, takers, and matchers all can—and do—achieve success. But there's something distinctive that happens when givers succeed: it spreads and cascades. When takers win, there's usually someone else who loses. Research shows that people tend to envy successful takers and look for ways to knock them down a notch. In contrast, when [givers] win, people are rooting for them and supporting them, rather than gunning for them. Givers succeed in a way that creates a ripple effect, enhancing the success of people around them.[9]

To maintain long-term bonds, we should strive to move from taking to matching and perhaps, even especially, giving. In the "Putting the Concept into Practice" section, we talk about how you can become a giver who lands at the top of the success ladder.

PUTTING THE CONCEPT INTO PRACTICE

The fear of being judged as weak or naïve prevents many people from operating like givers at work. [And yet, consider] when the average candidate was clumsy, audiences liked him even less. But when the expert was clumsy, audiences liked him even more.

—ADAM GRANT, *Give and Take*

The difference between the two types of givers is boundaries. The least successful givers say yes to everything and drop things they are working on to support others. This tends to make them sacrifice what is important to them, and they fall behind in their own work. By saying yes to one thing, they are inadvertently saying no to other things.

In contrast, successful givers appreciate their value and their time, create healthy boundaries, and seek to achieve a win-win-win outcome. As Grant shares:

> This is what I find most magnetic about successful givers: they get to the top without cutting others down, finding ways of expanding the pie that benefit themselves and the people around them. Whereas success is zero-sum in a group of takers, in groups of givers, it may be true that the whole is greater than the sum of the parts.[10]

With so many possible connections and relationships to build in our digital age, we might struggle significantly with establishing depth—and committing to maintaining that depth over a long time. That's why starting with choosing where to invest your time and energy is so important.

Think back to the three kinds of relationships from Edgar Schein's work that we shared earlier in this part. Is the relationship transactional, personal, or transformative? Evaluating our relationships with different people helps us know how much time and energy to put into giving. When engaging in a transactional relationship rather than a relational or transformative relationship, we can guard our time and resources to prevent ourselves from being overleveraged. Successful givers easily identify takers and protect their time and resources.

One technique used by successful givers, and a good time management tool, is the five-minute favor.[11] A five-minute favor is a favor you can do that takes you no more than five minutes to do. Some examples include:

- Give recognition via an email or meeting when someone does a good job.

- Use a product and offer concise, vivid, and helpful feedback.

- Introduce two people with a well-written email, citing a mutual interest.

- Read a summary and offer crisp and concrete feedback.

- Serve as a reference for a person, product, or service.

- Share, comment, or retweet something on social media.

THE 5 MINUTE FAVOR

Whether you choose to be a matcher or a giver, the idea is to help others without overextending yourself and becoming burned out. It's vital to treat giving as a marathon and reserve your energies for those who will support you in return as they become successful as a result of your support. Rather than being inconsistent (easy to do in our overwhelming world!), strive to have integrity and reliability in your relationships. You'll find significant rewards waiting for you.

A STEM METAPHOR TO DRIVE THE POINT HOME: SYMBIOSIS

In the science world, we know some species live through different forms of collaborative relationships. Some can be parasitic—taking what they need, regardless of the harm caused to the host. Others can engage in symbiotic relationships. Each species depends on the other and benefits through the interaction—sometimes their very lives depend on one another's success. Others can give regardless of getting anything back. In nature, just like in society, all three of these approaches are valid and successful. But symbiotic relationships tend to create more abundance in themselves and their environment, while parasitic ones only enhance their own survival.

A STORY IN ACTION

Elaine was a terrific team player. She showed up to each meeting excited about her job and helped her team thrive. Although busy with her work, she always found time to help others.

Late one Thursday afternoon, her colleague Robert stopped by her office to ask for her help. She was trying to leave the office in the next few minutes to meet with some friends but felt the need to help Robert. Given the aggressive timeline, he shared what he needed, and she agreed to help. On her way out of the office, she stopped at his office to ask a question.

She noticed his door was shut and locked. She asked Jake, whose office was next door, where Robert was. Jake answered that Robert had left for vacation and would be back on Monday. Elaine was upset because she was not only late to meet her friends but also now stuck doing Robert's work while he took a long weekend off.

Over the weekend, while working on Robert's project, Elaine understood that she loves helping others out. But the help she offered to Robert was chipping away at her time to enjoy life and do the things that keep her in a positive mood. She decided that starting with Robert's return to the office, she would set boundaries so she could feel good about helping other people without being taken advantage of.

REFLECTION QUESTIONS

- What makes you hold back from engaging fully in a relationship?

- Which category—giver, taker, matcher—do you think you fall into?

- How can you apply the reciprocity principle to grow stronger bonds in your relationships?

- What struggles have you faced in our remote digital world with forming relationships? What concerns or challenges you the most?

- Where do you think it would be most helpful to put your focus first? Here are some questions to consider:

  - To whom it is worth giving your energy?

  - Can you brainstorm some different ways you can give to other people?

  - How or why might you switch from a taking style to a giving or matching style?

FURTHER READING AND REFERENCES

On the more casual side . . . books and resources to check out:

Grant, Adam. (2013). *Give and Take: A Revolutionary Approach to Success.*

Scanlon, L. G., and A. Vernick. (2019). *Five Minutes: (That's a Lot of Time) (No, It's Not) (Yes, It Is).*

PART 3

$$N = \sum_{i-n}^{n} X_i$$

THE FIRST PRINCIPLES OF TEAM MEMBERSHIP

Membership in groups simultaneously creates fear and hope—fear that the group will be either overwhelming or isolating and hope that participation will be both personally and collectively enhancing.

—**SMITH AND BERG,** *Paradoxes of Group Life*

In the previous parts, we have built your tool kit for growing your self-awareness, becoming more intentional about your interactions, and navigating the dynamics of a relationship.

Now you might be thinking, "It's complex enough to deal with myself and one other person. What about when I am on a team of people?" Complexity Theory is a key principle that states that simple rules give rise to complex systems, and complex rules lead to simple systems. As we move forward, this thought may comfort you: Although we certainly create complex systems together, each of us is built on the simple ideas and concepts we shared in parts 1 and 2. Knowing and navigating yourself helps you know and navigate others.

This part will expand your understanding and tool kit to help you work through the typical challenges that arise in teamwork situations and make working on teams a fun part of your work life. This is important because most of us often have to work on teams. Consider the following situations:

- As part of a traditional team, your assignment might include being a part of a department or team within a department. This community is one you will engage with often and over an extended period of time. Your ability to build positive relationships here can significantly impact your future career growth and the career network that supports you.

- You may be invited to be on a short-term team where you engage with a project team that forms and then disbands after the project is over. In this situation, you might not have much time to get to know teammates and figure out how to become a high-functioning team member.

- As part of a remote team, whether a short-term or long-term team, you might not see the people you're working with and you may not ever meet face to face in this group. In return, they may not see you, either. Your ability to communicate, share yourself, and build bonds takes on new direction and importance.

- As part of a hybrid team, you might be in a team where some people are in person and others are not. You might be the one in the room, or you might be virtual. Either way, actively including people outside the room, even if that is yourself, in a manner that supports engagement at a level equal to those inside the room is an important skill set.

CONNECT BACK TO WHY

New technologies and solutions in the cloud are emerging every day, from artificial intelligence to blockchain to augmented reality to software as a service and more. These solutions have the potential to make life easier—and the potential to create barriers of entry for others. For example, at developers.google.com, developers are guided to write with inclusivity in mind, including avoiding "ableist language and gendered language" and to use diverse and inclusive examples.[1] When developing products to express yourself, knowledge of others and other points of view help you become a better STEM professional.

To help navigate these situations, this part includes the following topics:

- **EXPECTING REALISTIC PERFORMANCE (PAGE 109):** You will learn how teams develop over time and set realistic expectations.

- **BUILDING TEAM TRUST (PAGE 122):** You will learn about building trust in your team members and being trustworthy yourself.

- **BRINGING YOURSELF (PAGE 135):** You will learn how to create psychological safety in your team, so you and others feel safe to show up.

- **NAVIGATING CONFLICT (PAGE 145):** You will learn the Crucial Conversation method to navigate conflict.

- **LEVERAGING DIVERSITY (PAGE 156):** You will learn how to include team differences through polarity thinking.

3.1
EXPECTING REALISTIC PERFORMANCE | TEAM DEVELOPMENT LIFECYCLE

If you take out the team in teamwork, it's just work. Now who wants that?

—MATTHEW WOODRING STOVER

THE PROBLEM	• Do you get easily frustrated when a team first starts and isn't instantly productive?
These are just *some* of the challenges you might encounter that viewing performance through a lifecycle approach to team development helps solve.	• Do you struggle knowing how to jumpstart a team or get it unstuck?
	• Do you know where to begin with a new team?
	• Do you find that new team members hold back the team's progress?

Starting on a new team is never easy, even if you know the people on the team or they are your friends. In fact, being friends can make it harder sometimes! The team dynamics at play need to be explored for all team members to work effectively with others. That's because even if you know someone's life stories or have an individual connection, their work style and approach may be new to you—and can be different depending on what the situation is and what's going on for them in the Hidden area of their Johari Window.

The exciting thing about teams is that every time a new person joins a team, the team formation process starts over again, to some degree. This means that whether you are entering a new team or welcoming a new team member, you are likely to experience some tension, conflict, frustration, and (often) a lack of forward progress.

The roadblocks tend to be higher when you expect everything will be as it was or expect the team to be easy to get started. By understanding how teams develop over time and managing your own and others' expectations, you intentionally create space and effective action towards onboarding new team members and gelling together as a team more quickly.

For the team to get synchronized, team members must initially put in the work to form, grow, and find alignment. Many relationship issues occur initially, especially when expectations are high or goals and timelines are looming. You and your team might be tempted to skip healthy team formation steps—only to find that you wish you'd taken the time later on down the road. "Go slow to go fast" is a good rule of thumb to continue to keep in mind.

Understanding the typical stages teams go through can help you set realistic expectations, navigate frustration others might experience, and speed up towards high-functioning collaboration. The concept of team development, covered in this topic, is essential because organizations want you to drop in to a new group or team and get to productivity as rapidly as possible.

EXPECTING REALISTIC PERFORMANCE THROUGH THE TEAM DEVELOPMENT LIFECYCLE

Coming together is a beginning. Keeping together is progress. Working together is success.

—HENRY FORD

Organizational experts have many ways to describe how a team evolves. Here, we will explore two of the most often used concepts in team development. The first is a team development process of four stages attributed to Bruce Tuckman called forming, storming, norming, and performing.[2] The second concept is punctuated equilibrium, developed by organizational behavior expert Connie Gersick.[3]

Tuckman's four stages of team development describe a process in which the team comes together and works in stages to achieve an optimal level of performance. In this concept, the stages are sequential and the time spent in each stage varies in duration. However, unexpected setbacks might cause the team to revert back to a prior stage.

🙂🙂🙂🙂	FORMING
😠😠😠😠	STORMING
🙂😐🙂🙂	NORMING
🙂🙂🙂🙂	PERFORMING

- **FORMING STAGE:** In this stage, the most critical step is to create a team charter. A team charter outlines the purpose and goal of the team, general routine and communication expectations, roles, decision-making methods, timelines, expected and desired behavioral norms, and performance management processes (ways to measure whether the team is on or off track and management actions to take if the team is off track). The process of building a team charter helps reduce the storming stage and creates an optimal norming stage in which the team is prepared to perform more quickly. It's often the case that teams do *not* formally create a charter and suffer from misalignments in expectations later on.

- **STORMING STAGE:** The team deals with the transition from behaving independently to becoming interdependent for the task's success. Each person on a team has a style and process that takes time to integrate into a collective flow. This stage can have the most tension because team members may resist integration as the team tries to forge a collective identity. Team members might try to hold on to their personal identities by expressing their individuality, arguing their point of view, or insisting (indirectly or overtly) that their way is the only way. And they may indirectly or overtly express a low acceptance of others' ideas or a collective team approach. This resistance fades over time as team members gain experience working with each other's styles, build trust, and create clarity around the work.

- **NORMING STAGE:** This stage is about achieving team cohesion. Team cohesiveness is demonstrated through the adherence to the team charter and trust in collective ways of working, even if those differ from an individual member's norms. These collaborative ways of working are often formally noted as team norms, but sometimes operate as unwritten rules. These norms could include everything from standard meeting times to naming principles or priorities to guide decision-making. Also, in this stage, team members transform their desire for success into team success. These shared attitudes and beliefs advance the team into the last stage, performing.

- **PERFORMING STAGE:** During this stage, the team operates on shared attitudes, beliefs, and practices to constructively problem-solve to accomplish given tasks. Often, this is the stage where you feel you're enjoying your team members and feeling like you are all making progress.

Another way of looking at team development is Gersick's Punctuated Equilibrium Model.[4] This approach shifts the focus from internal team structure to dealing with forces external to the team. Punctuated equilibrium describes a linear process where the team is in equilibrium until they face pressures that radically change the trajectory of the team's goals.

Three stages explain the team's response and resulting growth. The duration between these stages fluctuates wildly between different teams.

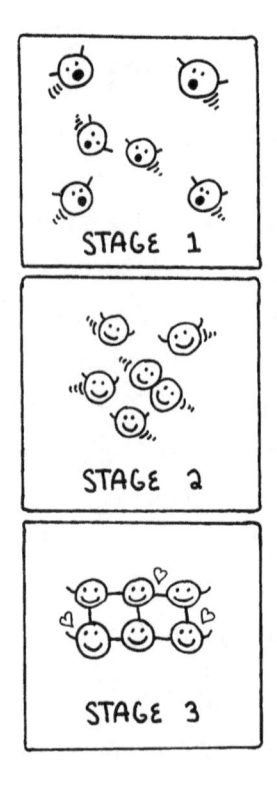

- Stage 1 is a more relaxed and highly socialized period since completing tasks is far in the future. The team is forming and defining the team's goals. The team is characterized by a lack of urgency, low performance, and relatively high inertia.

- Then Stage 2, a radical change, forces the team to show a sense of urgency and work on the task with significant energy. Perhaps the deadline is looming closer, or a resource the team has been waiting on has arrived. Performance shifts to high gear, and each member may not share the same sense of urgency. During this flux in coordination, the team members' interactions are unpredictable and can cause tension and anxiety. Roles, attitudes, and behaviors shift while working through this disequilibrium. The higher the level of flux during Stage 2, the more disturbing effect the change has on the team, and the more the team has to grow together to get back to equilibrium. After the punctuational change is experienced and stability is regained, the team enters a new phase, Stage 3.

- In Stage 3, the team enters a revolutionary period with redefined next steps. Unsuccessful patterns are broken, new perspectives are adopted, and new directions and goals are established.

Though these models provide logic to team development, don't discount the powerful emotions underlying each phase. Whether your team is storming or adapting to a radical change, each individual genuinely struggles with the notion of joining a group. Why? In *Paradoxes of Group Life*, Kenwyn Smith and David Berg explain that simply being part of a group involves facing many contradictions that feel like impossible either/or choices: "Groups are pervaded by a wide range of emotions, thoughts, and actions that their members experience as contradictory, and that the attempts to unravel these contradictory forces create a circular process that is paralyzing to groups."[5]

In the book *Becoming Human*, Jean Vanier points out one specific contradiction related to our strong desire for individuality:

> As humans we are caught up between competing drives, the drive to belong, to fit in and be a part of something bigger than ourselves, and the drive to let our deepest selves rise up, to walk alone, to refuse the accepted and the comfortable. In each one of us, there is a shadow side, which, from time to time, manifests itself in our consciousness through anger, frustration, or depression, through the refusal to belong, because belonging appears to be something that crushes freedom.[6]

No wonder we need time to develop as a team as we each individually decide how we will work with others! It's unrealistic to expect a team to function right away. These two team development concepts offer insights into how teams develop and become functioning groups. Neither concept is necessarily better than the other—you can think of the teams you are on and which concept resonates with you more. Whichever model you choose in the moment, it can help your team members understand where they are in their team's evolution and give them language to express what they are experiencing. Now, your team members can have a shared awareness to help identify when misalignment is going on and where you might need to spend more time as a team to figure out your working process.

PUTTING THE CONCEPT INTO PRACTICE

The enemy of accountability is ambiguity.

—**PATRICK LENCIONI,** *The Five Dysfunctions of a Team*

One of the most common causes of conflict in teams is when someone expects someone else to do something, and it doesn't happen. But often, the expectation was never made clear in the first place!

When joining or welcoming a new team member, start with the team chartering process. Ensure all the new and existing team members understand how teams develop and provide ways to deal with the different stages of team development to bring the team members closer together.

A team charter is a documented set of expectations that is often the output of a team kickoff meeting. This can be as formal as filling out a standard template but can be as informal as a set of bullet points captured as meeting notes. Regardless of the level of formality, here are some questions to help your team solidify the purpose and expected outcomes of the team.

- What is the purpose of our work together?
- What goals do we want to set?
- What timeline do we want to set?
- What key milestones and tasks will get us to our goal?
- How do we want to work with one another?
- Who will take on what role/responsibility?
- How will we keep one another accountable to deliver on our responsibilities?

- How frequently should we meet?
- How will we know whether we are successful?
- What metric can we use to measure our success?

A STEM METAPHOR TO DRIVE THE POINT HOME: GENERAL SYSTEMS THEORY

General Systems Theory suggests that the whole is greater than the sum of its parts. In a study of General Systems Theory in engineering, Fleming Ray states, "This systems approach arose in contrast to the Newtonian method of separating an object into its component parts and trying to understand the behavior of the object by understanding the properties of the individual parts while ignoring their interactions."[7]

The same concept applies to working in teams. Even though each individual brings something distinct, together the members of a team might combine or collide in unexpected ways. Rather than keeping these collisions under the surface, General Systems Theory implies that naming and actively working with the whole is more effective. It makes sense that these interactions wouldn't be evident from the outset but may take time to discover and leverage effectively.

A STORY IN ACTION

Imagine you just joined a team. How well do you know the people on the team? You've worked with a few of the other team members in the past. You recall that some of their work styles worked well for you but others not so much. And some people are brand new to you.

- Harry did a great job last time but tended to work

independently. He's brilliant when he is immersed in his task, but because he wasn't engaged during meetings, you weren't sure if he was working on anything at all.

- Temi struck you as concerned about time . . . all the time. Whenever the team was getting deeper into the details of a specific task, Temi sounded impatient and wanted to move to the next step, even though the team clearly wasn't ready to move on yet.

- Sarah is a new person for you, but in the first meeting, she jumped in right way and made efforts to contribute. Her eagerness could be a good thing, but you aren't sure yet.

Knowing that teams develop over time, you decide to approach this project differently than you approached previous projects. When Temi throws the schedule up on the screen, you suggest stepping back and talking about how you each work and how you all might want to work together. By the end of the first call, the schedule is addressed—but so is a document containing a draft set of norms for working together, including how to communicate, the frequency of communication, strengths of each team member, which tasks are preferred (or not preferred) by various team members, and other aspects on working styles.

REFLECTION QUESTIONS

- Consider the teams you're on currently. Which team development model speaks to you? What stage would you say your teams are at?

- How often have you been on a team where there was a formal process at the beginning to agree on goals and work process norms? Was it helpful? Why or why not?

- Reflecting on your teamwork, where do you think your team struggled the most when just starting to work together? How about now? Do you have clarity on roles, schedule, working norms, or other common issues that can cause misalignments and become roadblocks to productivity?

- Knowing what you know now, how might you call attention to any misalignments in expectations and encourage your team to take a step back and create a charter?

- What expectations do you have for yourself and your team members?

- How well do your team members know your expectation of them?

FURTHER READING AND REFERENCES

On the more casual side . . . books and resources to check out:

Lencioni, Patrick. (2002). *The Five Dysfunctions of a Team.*

Vanier, Jean. (2008). *Becoming Human.*

On the more academic side . . . references we used:

Ray, Fleming. (2000). "General Systems Theory: A Knowledge Domain in Engineering Systems."

https://studylib.net/doc/18760994/general-systems-theory-a-knowledge-domain-in.

Gersick, Connie. (1988). "Time and Transition in Work Teams: Toward a New Model of Group Development." *Academy of Management Journal.* https://doi.org/10.5465/256496.

Smith, Kenwyn K., and David N. Berg. (1997). *Paradoxes of Group Life: Understanding Conflict, Paralysis, and Movement in Group Dynamics.*

Tuckman, B. W. (1965). "Developmental Sequence in Small Groups." *Psychological Bulletin.* https://doi.org/10.1037/h0022100.

3.2

BUILDING TEAM TRUST | COVEY'S SPEED OF TRUST MODEL

Low trust is the highest predictor of re-work—wasted time spent redoing a task. When trust is lacking, we spend so much time and energy covering our bases, protecting our turf, and creating alliances that we can't do anything effectively.

—RICHARD FAGERLIN, *Trustology*

A team is not a group of people who work together. A team is a group of people who trust each other.

—SIMON SINEK

Building Team Trust | Covey's Speed of Trust Model | 123

THE PROBLEM	• Do you or your team members struggle to be open with thoughts, motives, and ideas?
These are just *some* of the challenges you might encounter that building team trust helps solve.	• Do you often wonder whether people are working in alignment with the team goals or with their own goals?
	• Do you wonder whether your team members "have your back" and would support you when needed?
	• Do you wonder whether your team members will follow through on their commitments?

Have you ever thought about how much we trust systems, processes, and other people throughout the day? When driving, we trust people to stop at the stop sign. We trust the lights to come on when we flip the switch. And we trust our employers to pay us at every pay period. For the most part, we extend trust quite liberally. But the higher the perceived importance, rewards, and risk involved, the more cautious we become. In some ways, due to the limited ability of strangers to impact your life, it can be easier to trust them than to trust the people we work and live with every day! Consistent or high exposure to a person increases the risk that a mistake will happen that hurts our trust.

MY PLAN

REALITY

We start to experience distrust when we experience inconsistency between our expectations and the actual situation. And, since our expectations and people's responses can both vary drastically depending on the case, there is a lot of room for inconsistency. With many moving parts, if left unaddressed either as individuals or together as a team, we soon distrust anything or anyone who doesn't show consistency.

This sense of distrust shapes our internal mental models and how we interact with others. For example, you and another team member are taking on more work than the others. You and your team might expect that everyone should do equal work. This violation of expectations, and thus trust, is called into question. You might wonder how much you can trust your team members to do their part. Should we be prepared to fill in the gaps every time our team members don't step up? Is that fair?

Building trust between all team members is a vital part of team development. We might laugh at the cheesy team-building activities many of us have participated in. But we can all easily name the consequences of distrust—and those consequences tend to be costly and high. In the concept below, we explain how to build trust by creating a shared awareness of what has happened in the past, what is happening now, and coordinating what to do in the future.

BUILDING TEAM TRUST THROUGH COVEY'S SPEED OF TRUST MODEL

We judge ourselves by our intentions and others by their behavior. A person has integrity when there is no gap between intent and behavior . . . when he or she is whole, seamless, the same—inside and out. I call this "congruence." And it is congruence—not compliance—that will ultimately create credibility and trust. This is why one of the fastest ways to restore trust is to make and keep commitments—even very small commitments—to ourselves and to others.

—STEPHEN COVEY, *The Speed of Trust*

As we discussed in the "Inviting People In" and "Growing Long-Term Bonds" topics, consistency is key to successful one-on-one relationships. The same idea becomes exponentially necessary when we talk about teams—and not just one-on-one with your favorite team member, but with all team members as a whole. Anyone who has been involved in a group with cliques or side conversations knows the difference between team members trusting each other and having the entire team trust. In this topic, let's go deeper into consistency as the means for building trust for a whole team.

We can think of trust as being confident that people will behave consistently with our mental model and the situation. Therefore, to trust is to take a risk by putting confidence in the reliability of another—and being able to depend on the reliability of another is what a team is. Rather than focusing on our individual narrative and expectations (remember the Ladder of Inference?), trust develops when team members evolve and recognize their interdependencies, individual behaviors, task activities, and situational factors. As Richard Fagerlin says in his book, *Trustology*:

> Trust cannot be earned; it can only be given. When we insist on keeping score, everyone loses. Since it's impossible to keep score, it's time to submit your resignation letter as the referee of your relationships. Time to stop keeping tabs of who is ahead in thoughtful, trust-earning behavior.[8]

SCALE OF TRUST

- Competency: results, capability
- Character: intent, integrity

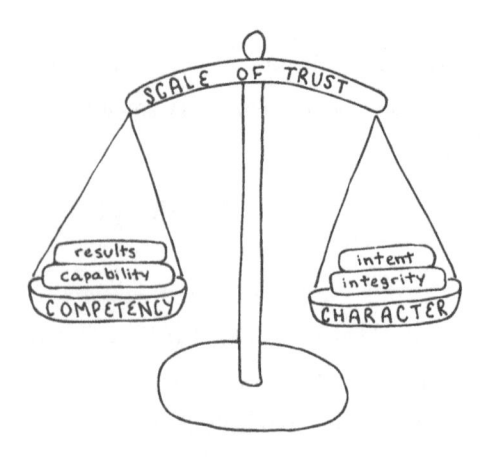

If you're no longer keeping score and counting who is doing what to earn your trust, then how do you decide whether to trust people and who to trust? Stephen Covey distills trust down to two dimensions in his book *The Speed of Trust*: We need to trust people for their character and their competency.

- **CHARACTER:** Refers to our *integrity* (honesty, fairness, authenticity) and *intent* (motives, transparency, behaviors). It's about really knowing who we are and consistently behaving in a way that aligns with those values so that people can observe and determine whether they can reliably trust our character. This dimension of trust is important to self-reflect on because you can't give what you don't have. If you don't trust yourself, the chances of you trusting others are unlikely. You also cannot expect others to trust you if you behave in an untrustworthy manner. There might be inconsistencies between your integrity and intentions. This could come about for a variety of reasons. Nevertheless, by self-discovering the gap and making incremental shifts to close the gap, you can achieve both self-trust and the extension of trust.

- **COMPETENCY:** Covey breaks down competency to *capability* (skill, knowledge, expertise) and *results* (reputation, credibility, performance). Our competency is what landed us on the team in the first place. We were able to demonstrate both our capability and our results. It's important to think of these two as equals, meaning if you are capable but do not show the results, the inconsistency would create a level of distrust. Imagine someone you know who is undoubtedly brilliant but chooses not to contribute fully to the team. Do you have much trust in this individual? Conversely, if you show results but not the capability, others might not trust that you were the one who put in the work. And remember, if you are not trusted for who you are (your character), the chances of being trusted for what you do are low.

Although these two dimensions don't always have to be 100 percent perfect for trust to develop, in some cases you won't trust the person because of inconsistency in their character. Yet, you trust that they will get the job done because they are competent and have their own motivation to succeed. These types of inconsistencies can influence our evaluation of people in general and can soon develop into a habit of an if/then approach to trust.

Rather than assuming 100 percent perfect trustworthy behavior as the goal, Kenwyn Smith and David Berg's *Paradoxes of Group Life* suggests focusing on the process of trusting as a way to break through the familiar vicious cycle of distrust:

> Group life is filled with dilemmas in which one needs to trust others but where the development of trust depends on the trust already existing. However, if a group and its individual

members trust that the individual and collective feedback processes, operating in tandem, provide the possibility for self-correction and growth... Then, the issue of trust has been changed to one of the trusting that which seems untrustable and discovering that engaging in the process of trusting, rather than the content of the trust, creates a group in which people feel increasingly safe disclosing the weak and the ugly.[9]

It's important to think about these concepts when it comes to trusting another individual and building trust together as a team.

PUTTING THE CONCEPT INTO PRACTICE

There are two parts to a high-trust relationship. You must trust them, and they must trust you. Both are your responsibility. Why? You can't control the other person's willingness to trust. You can't control whether or not they are trustworthy. But you can control yourself. When you are the truster, you are responsible to give trust, without knowing if you'll get anything back. When you are the trustee, the person wanting to be trusted, you are responsible to show yourself trustworthy.

—RICHARD FAGERLIN, *Trustology*

You might think it's on "them" to create trust. But as Fagerlin eloquently puts it, both trusting and being trustworthy are your job. Here are some perspectives on how you can actively generate trust during teamwork.

At the beginning of team formation, you can create dialogue that asks people to share their character and competency. You can find many team-building activities online.

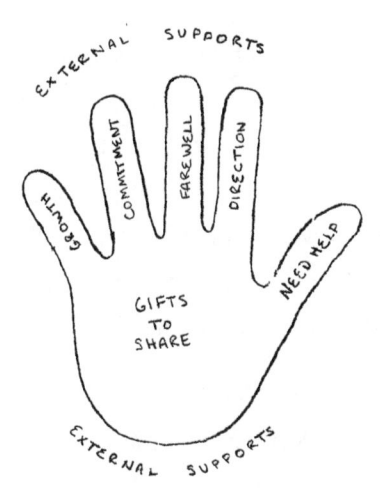

As an example, here's a simple activity called "In the Palm of My Hand" (anonymous source). In this activity, each team member traces their hand on a paper, fills out these questions, and then takes a picture of their work to discuss and share.

1. **PINKY (OR LITTLE) FINGER:** What is one growing edge that you'd like to attend to during the course of this experience?

2. **FOURTH FINGER:** In some cultures, this is a finger of commitment. What commitment are you willing to make to yourself / to the group / to your team?

3. **MIDDLE FINGER:** We sometimes use this finger to bid the proverbial farewell to unpleasant experiences or moments. What is a limiting belief, thought, or experience that you're ready to say goodbye to?

4. **INDEX FINGER:** We often use this finger to indicate and give direction. Where are you headed? In what direction are you moving / do you wish to proceed?

5. **THUMB:** Option 1: Hitchhikers sometimes display their thumb to indicate that they need assistance. What is something that you'd currently like help with from this group / from others? Option 2: The thumb allows us to grip and hold on to things tightly. What do you want to hold on to during this experience? Or in other words, what do you want to make sure not to let go of during this experience?

6. **AREA AROUND THE HAND:** What external supports currently exist around you (people, practices, hobbies, etc.)?

7. **THE PALM OF THE HAND:** Which of your gifts are you willing to offer/give/share with others?

Many activities like this one can help build trust at the beginning of the team formation process. However, what do you do when you've already started working together and you notice a pattern of mistrust? An easy way to assess whether trust is the problem is shared by Stephen Covey: "In a high-trust relationship, you can say the wrong thing, and people will still get your meaning. In a low-trust relationship, you can be very measured, even precise, and they'll still misinterpret you."[10]

When sensing inconsistencies or mistrust, first remember that human beings are often inconsistent by nature. We like to think we always behave a certain way, but the reality is there is always a variation of that "always" behavior. When running into issues of trust, consider the following approach to applying Covey's Speed of Trust concept:

1. As a team, do you all trust one another? Are there specific individuals you or the team at large mistrusts?

2. Take a closer look at the mistrust. Where do you feel the inconsistency in relying on others or those individuals? Is it in their character or their competency, or both?

3. If it's in their character, is it related more to their integrity, intent, or both?

4. If it's in their competency, is it related to their capability, results, or both?

5. Thinking back on team development, consider the following questions:

    a. Are there new working norms or team values the team could discuss together to create clarity around expectations?

    b. Do the goals or charter of the team need to be revisited? What about roles and tasks?

    c. Beyond process, is the lack of trust caused by interpersonal issues, a lack of understanding motives, or clashes of personality? What team or individual bonding activities might widen the Open square of the Johari Window?

Whether you are building trust for the first time, developing it with an existing team, or addressing an issue in the moment, the Covey Speed of Trust model and crafting activities for your team can help.

A STEM METAPHOR TO DRIVE THE POINT HOME: THE LAW OF UNINTENDED CONSEQUENCES

One aspect of the engineering design process is the law of unintended consequences. The law of unintended consequences states that there is an unintended or unanticipated outcome for every action. In engineering design, possible results can be anticipated but are sometimes intentionally ignored or are disregarded because of the need to make trade-offs against other design decisions. The unanticipated and unintended consequences are often caused by a lack of organization, where individuals have their own goals apart from the team.

Although conventional thinking suggests that we don't know what we don't know, there is a growing need to broaden our understanding of the responsibilities of a technical professional. When team members trust one another and watch out for one another, it is more likely that previously ignored possible outcomes will be brought to the surface because members will feel safer and share their observations and thoughts. Assessing those possible outcomes will help the team reach their positive, intended consequences. Our results (competency) must be congruent with our intentions (character) to build trust.

A STORY IN ACTION

Phillip, Jacob, Tamara, Jessie, and Laree were part of a high-profile project. They worked with one another for a short time and were still storming and norming in the team development process. Tamara and Jessie communicated about inconsistencies in the project design and shared their concerns about successfully reaching the team goal. As the newest members, they were encouraged to trust the process.

As time passed, Jacob began to question his trust for Phillip. As the senior researcher on the team, Phillip was under a substantial amount of pressure. But that was no excuse for the way he treated team members unfairly. Phillip's drive for results was creating a deviation from the team charter they had developed in the beginning.

Tamara, Jessie, and Jacob brought up the inconsistencies at the next team meeting, and they found they had difficulty trusting the team's process. After much dialogue, Phillip realized he was acting out of character because he felt pressure to design a flawless system.

Through the remaining months of the project, the team was able to bring up the inconsistencies in each other's character or competency. It wasn't always easy, but the more the team committed to doing this, the more trust and safety it could build. This allowed the team members to challenge one another to design a flawless system with sufficient backups to mitigate potential flaws.

REFLECTION QUESTIONS

- Where do you sense your team is with its levels of trust?
- Where are you personally with trusting others on your team?
- Where are you personally with trusting yourself?
- How would you like to contribute to building trust on your team and in your relationships?
- Would you say you behave in a consistent, reliable manner in both of the trust dimensions?
- What can you do to grow trust in yourself? In others? What small commitments will you make?

FURTHER READING AND REFERENCES

On the more casual side . . . books and resources to check out:

Covey, Stephen M. R. (2006). *The Speed of Trust: The One Thing That Changes Everything.*

Fagerlin, Richard. (2013). *Trustology: The Art and Science of Leading High-Trust Teams.*

On the more academic side . . . a reference we used:

Smith, Kenwyn K., and David N. Berg. (1997). *Paradoxes of Group Life: Understanding Conflict, Paralysis, and Movement in Group Dynamics.*

3.3

BRINGING YOURSELF | PSYCHOLOGICAL SAFETY

Silence rarely announces itself. The moment passes, and no one is the wiser except the person who held back.

—**AMY EDMONDSON,** on the *People and Projects Podcast*

THE PROBLEM These are just *some* of the challenges you might encounter that creating psychological safety helps solve.	• Do you or your team members struggle to be open with thoughts, motives, and ideas? • Do you feel unsafe being vulnerable and imperfect with your team? Do you always feel pressure to be right? • Do you notice one or two members dominating the groups and others remaining silent? Do you sense that conversations are being shut down? • Does your team quickly center on an idea rather than open it for discussion and brainstorming? • Do you feel like people (including you) are bringing their whole selves to the team? Or are you all spending a lot of time covering up personal information?

Even though you might trust your team to complete tasks together, that may not mean that you feel your team is psychologically safe. Have you ever felt afraid to ask a question and share your perspective, especially when it's clearly a bit different from what the others are saying? Have you ever felt unappreciated for what you contribute? Having psychological safety means having a low level of fear and a sense of trust in the team environment—trusting that if you take risks, you will not suffer negative consequences. When team members create a psychologically safe environment, they promote curiosity, collaboration, comfort with showing vulnerability and asking for help, and a learning environment.

For example, walking into or logging into a virtual meeting might not always feel like the safest environment, especially on new teams or when high risks are at stake. You might not know who will attend, what is on the agenda, or where some conversations will go. It could also be a listen-only meeting in which dominant voices in the meeting don't allow airtime for others to share. As uncomfortable as it might be to walk into a meeting in general, it's even more painful when you don't feel safe around your team members.

Suppose the team's culture does not readily accept asks for help or learning by making mistakes. In that case, you may be afraid that important information or barriers will be hidden during the meeting and that calling attention to team needs will create consequences for you personally. If the team culture is more critical, knocking one another down rather than building one another up, you might be afraid that no one will back you up if you speak up during the meeting. In short, you may feel like your point of view is not welcome, and rather than bringing it to the table, you will spend your energy trying to fit into the norm and hiding any alternative approaches or thoughts.

To reduce unsafe feelings for you and build a team norm around psychological safety, we will explore a concept called *interpersonal risk*.

BRINGING YOURSELF BY CREATING PSYCHOLOGICAL SAFETY

When we commit to connect, we are letting go of who we should be in order to be who we are.

—BRENÉ BROWN

Psychological safety is being "able to show and employ oneself without fear of negative consequences of self-image, status or career."[11] As simple as the concept might sound, it's tough to create. That's because in a diverse team, what might feel safe for you could create an unsafe environment for another. While that might not be our intention, we are all guilty of contributing to an unsafe environment by being different and having different ways of thinking and communicating.

For example, consider a time someone brought up a suggestion that you disagreed with. You might have just sat there and said nothing, or you might have suggested a different idea. These nonverbal and verbal responses created a potential negative feeling. The other person may now feel that it is not safe to share their ideas during future interactions with you. While you felt psychologically safe withholding or expressing your thoughts, another person might not have had the same experience. Therefore, it can actually be counterproductive to create psychological safety for yourself if you do not also create psychological safety for others.

One way to create the most significant amount of psychological safety for everyone on the team is to consider interpersonal risk. Interpersonal risk is negatively related to psychological safety. This means that as risk goes up, safety goes down, and vice versa. Interpersonal risk acknowledges that every situation, action, conversation, or suggestion we make comes with a certain amount of risk to our social and professional standing with others. The ultimate goal of psychological safety is to protect everyone from any harm.

All relationships, especially professional ones, won't work unless they are protected and nurtured. Here are few concepts to help protect and nurture relationships.

- Seek to get in front of situations that you anticipate will increase interpersonal risks. Use the SCARF model to help set those situations up for success.

- Decrease risk in the moment by not taking others' pushback or different ideas personally (see topic 2.3).

- Push through uncomfortable moments in a conversation by using inquiry (see topic 1.4) about what the other person means or how you could communicate your idea so it makes sense to them.

- The more you create space for everyone in the conversation to have an equal amount of time to share, the more you will create safety for yourself and others.

PUTTING THE CONCEPT INTO PRACTICE

First, you have to start with yourself and be honest about how psychologically safe it is to be around you. Check yourself for behaviors that might increase interpersonal risk. In the book *Permission to Speak Freely*, the authors share the following questions:

> Ask yourself:
> Do I welcome a spirit of speaking freely?
> Do I really welcome it?
> Let those questions echo within you for a few seconds. Do you want to hear the questions and uncertainties that the people you lead wish they could say, want to say, aren't sure they should say, feel vulnerable saying, and hold back from bringing up simply because they can't find the right words?[12]

If you've taken a hard look at yourself, you might be ready to take a look at how you as an individual operate in a team. Amy Edmonson, a pioneer of the psychological safety concept, shares the following statements as a way to measure how safe your team might be. Consider the statements and evaluate how strongly you agree or disagree. You can even do this as a team activity, where each individual provides their assessment, and then the team discusses together.

1. If you make a mistake on this team, it is often held against you.

2. Members of this team can bring up problems and challenging issues.

3. People on this team sometimes reject others for being different.

4. It is safe to take a risk on this team.

5. It is difficult to ask other members of this team for help.

6. No one on this team would deliberately act in a way that undermined my efforts.

7. Among members of this team, my unique skills and talents are valued and utilized.

Psychological safety is a highly complex topic, and these tips are just a small starting point to help build momentum.

A STEM METAPHOR TO DRIVE THE POINT HOME: SAFETY ENGINEERING

Safety engineering is an applied science associated with system engineering. In safety engineering, the purpose is to ensure that a life-critical system continues as needed even when other pieces fail. It's a risk management approach to prevent accidents since it is hard to document and study near-miss incidents.

The discipline relies on a collection of professionals who actively give input to prevent accidents from happening. To be successful, the professionals have to accept risks and call into question when something is not right without being judged by their colleagues. In the same vein, when working on a team, we all need to be safety engineers and protect the psychological safety of one another. We need to be vulnerable to the possibility of being wrong or different; this approach will help us increase psychological safety for ourselves and our team members.

A STORY IN ACTION

Jered hosted this month's team meeting. He drafted the agenda and sent it to the team an hour before the meeting. This didn't give anyone the chance to review, add, or update the agenda with items they wanted to discuss. Independently, Beverly and Zack reached out to Jered with some things they wanted to share at the meeting. Jered didn't reply to their agenda emails but replied to other less time-sensitive and important emails. Walking into the room, Beverly and Zack (who didn't know they were both in a similar situation) weren't feeling very good about the meeting.

Jered started the meeting at the top of the agenda and didn't ask questions or open it up for others to add items. He gave little space for anyone to jump into the conversation or respond to what felt like a lecture.

Halfway into the meeting, Carlos raised his hand to cut Jered off. Jered picked up on the awkwardness of a person raising their hand and asked, "Carlos, do you have something to add?"

Carlos said, "I'm not sure if this is an okay time to raise this, but I'm not following some items you have brought up. I'm wondering if anyone has any reactions to what you've shared or if you plan on providing space for discussion later."

Jered was surprised—how could Carlos not follow such a terrific agenda accompanied by a stellar PowerPoint? The vulnerability Carlos showed, which was risky, created space for Beverly, Zack, and the others to share their voices. From that point to the end of the meeting, the team had a terrific dialogue:

- They revisited some of the items Jered had shared and addressed questions and ideas they each had.

- They shared other items to add to the agenda, for this meeting or the next. This way, things that Jered may not have realized were important did not get missed, and they stayed on track with their project schedule.

- They also talked about a better process in the future for meetings. They acknowledged Jered's work on the agenda and discussed how to create space for additions and dialogues.

Overall, they learned from one another, so they were better equipped to support one another. The team also made sure not to blame Jered for his mistake and instead used it as a learning opportunity for everyone.

Later that afternoon, Jered reflected on how his approach was leveraging *power over* versus his true intent of *power with*. He noticed that by having the responsibility of hosting the meeting, he had gone a little too far. He felt the pressure of having to have all the information and carry the whole meeting agenda. He realized that as a result of this pressure, he had dominated his fellow team members and had not shared the load and power.

REFLECTION QUESTIONS

- Have you worked on growing your power within? Do you feel confident in your views and your ability or willingness to take up space with others? Or is it easy to feel that your ideas are not as good as others?

- How psychologically safe do you feel with your team?

- How psychologically safe do you think others on the team feel? Consider using Edmonson's questions as a team exercise.

- What power plays are in motion with your team?

- How does your behavior show power within, with, to, and over? Do you tend towards one power dynamic more than others?

- What is one step you'd like to take to foster more psychological safety when people interact with you one-on-one? With your team as a whole?

FURTHER READING AND REFERENCES

On the more casual side . . . books and resources to check out:

Brown, Brené. (2010). "The Power of Vulnerability." https://www.ted.com/talks/brene_brown_the_power_of_vulnerability?language=en.

Edmondson, Amy. (November 28, 2018). "Do This to Help Your Project Team Learn, Innovate, and Grow, with Harvard Professor of Leadership Amy C. Edmondson." https://peopleandprojectspodcast.com/index.php/en/podcast-episodes/502-ppp-236-do-this-to-help-your-project-team-learn-innovate-and-grow-with-harvard-professor-of-leadership-amy-c-edmondson.html.

Edmondson, Amy. (June 18, 2019). "Psychological Safety." https://whitneyjohnson.com/amy-edmondson.

re:Work. (2022). "Tool: Foster Psychological Safety." (References Amy Edmonson's questionnaire.) https://rework.withgoogle.com/guides/understanding-team-effectiveness/steps/foster-psychological-safety.

Stuart, Graeme. (February 1, 2019). "4 Types of Power: What Are Power Over; Power With; Power To and Power Within?" https://sustainingcommunity.wordpress.com/2019/02/01/4-types-of-power.

On the more academic side . . . references we used:

Edmonson, Amy. (2018). *The Fearless Organization: Creating Psychological Safety in the Workplace for Learning, Innovation, and Growth.*

Kahn, W. A. (1990). "Psychological Conditions of Personal Engagement and Disengagement at Work." *Academy of Management Journal.* https://doi.org/10.2307/256287

Crandall, Doug, and Matt Kincaid. (2017). *Permission to Speak Freely: How the Best Leaders Cultivate a Culture of Candor.*

3.4

NAVIGATING CONFLICT | CRUCIAL CONVERSATIONS MODEL

When two people do not get along, it is easiest to say that their "personalities clash." However, attributing team conflict to personality clashes is not helpful and in fact, often makes things worse, since the only way to resolve the problem would be to get someone to change his or her personality.

—DYER, DYER, AND DYER, *Team Building*

THE PROBLEM	• Do you or your team members avoid conflict?
These are just *some* of the challenges you might encounter that using the Crucial Conversations model helps solve.	• Do you or your team members lack the skills to have healthy conflict?
	• Are conflicts viewed as unfavorable or harmful situations by your team?
	• Have past conflicts lingered below the surface of your team relationships?

Imagine sitting in a team meeting, and one of your team members brings up an idea you told him about the other day. He spoke about the concept as if it were his original idea, not yours. You reflected on the conversation and could clearly remember the place, time, and situation where the conversation took place. Rather than jumping up the Ladder of Inference right away and assuming negative intent, you approach your colleague after the meeting. You ask him whether he remembers you telling him this idea. He replies, "You never told me that. I don't recall you raising that idea. Why does it matter? We are on a team." You think to yourself, "What happened?" You feel angry, frustrated, and have a general sense that something isn't right and you don't want to work with him in the future. Now you have a conflict with a team member.

Many things could cause a conflict during teamwork, and personality isn't the root cause to focus on. Communication mishaps are breeding grounds for conflict that derail the team's process and can lead to one of three different dynamics of conflict:[13]

- **DYADIC:** Between two members.
- **INTRAGROUP:** Within the team.
- **INTERGROUP:** Between your team and another team.

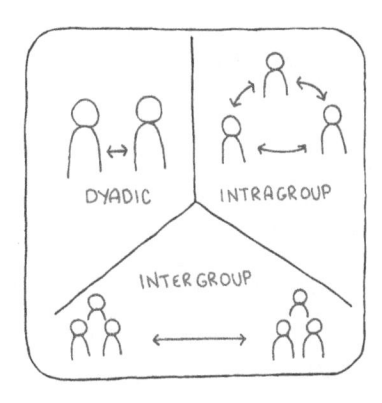

[Figure: Three types of conflict — DYADIC, INTRAGROUP, INTERGROUP]

Out of the three, the intragroup conflict is the most draining because it includes conflict about the overall team's task, process, and relationships. When intragroup or team conflict is clearly and quickly addressed, it helps the team members regain productivity, regain effectiveness, and resume their previous level of engagement. If left unaddressed, it could lead to more conflict, making it harder to regain a positive team culture. Often, once a team knows how to navigate conflict well, conflict becomes a healthy way to grow. This topic introduces a way to clearly and effectively address conflict: the Crucial Conversations model.

NAVIGATING CONFLICT BY LEADING CRUCIAL CONVERSATIONS

We often associate conflict with negative feelings and outcomes, which usually occur when we mishandle or avoid conflict. However, when we address conflict, we can turn a conflict situation from dysfunctional to functional and provide better opportunities to reach mutual agreements and generate better ideas. One way to tap into a valuable part of the conflict is to engage in a crucial conversation.

Crucial Conversations,[14] a concept developed by Kerry Patterson and colleagues, happen when the content of the interaction shifts from casual conversation to include:

1. Clearly differing opinions

2. High stakes

3. Potent emotions

Think about it. When you've disagreed with someone, you likely had one or more of the above three elements at play in the situation. Recognizing and knowing how to handle crucial conversations is vital for your skill set, team development, and trust and safety. As the authors say in the book:

> Could the ability to master crucial conversations help your career? Absolutely. For instance, high performers know how to stand up to their boss without committing career suicide. As it turns out, you don't have to choose between being honest and being effective. You don't have to choose between candor and your career. People who routinely hold crucial conversations and hold them well are able to express controversial and even risky opinions in a way that gets heard. Their bosses, peers, and direct reports listen without becoming defensive or angry.[15]

The Crucial Conversations methodology is a tool to manage conflict by exposing the elements that undermine a trustworthy and safe environment. Its goal is to get people to step back from the discussion to reveal all the relevant information and meaning behind clashing ideas, uncertainty, and emotions. The authors explain that "at the core of every successful conversation lies the free flow of relevant information. When it comes to risky, controversial, and emotional conversations, skilled people find a way to get all relevant information (from themselves and others) out into the open."[16] It's a dialogue about our concerns and fears that impacts the direction of the team. Simply put, it strongly encourages all of us to acknowledge that we have our own narratives about a conflict and that we care enough to align those narratives.

To mentally prepare for a crucial conversation, we need to exercise mindfulness and create a pause. Mindfulness offers us the space to be present in the moment without judgment. We can hear the concerns or fears others are voicing by being present and listening. By suspending judgment on what others are sharing and by not racing up the Ladder of Inference, we learn to silence our internal conversations and shift our focus to the external discussion between team members. We also need a high degree of self-awareness, and we need to know what our Fatal Fears might be, so we can let go of what isn't helpful rather than reacting and harming others.

With each crucial conversation, we get better at unearthing the different underlying opinions, becoming aligned on what and how much is really at stake, and navigating the emotions that come with the interaction. As we engage in more crucial conversations, we turn conflict into a competitive advantage by employing it as a functional conflict in which we find the most meaningful solutions. In the "Putting the Concept into Practice" section, we share an overview of the steps of the model.

PUTTING THE CONCEPT INTO PRACTICE

When two or more of us enter crucial conversations, our opinions differ. People who are skilled at dialogue do their best to make it safe for everyone to add their meaning to the shared pool—even ideas that at first glance appear controversial, wrong, or at odds with their own beliefs. Now obviously they don't agree with every idea; they simply do their best to ensure all ideas find their way into the open.

—**KERRY PATTERSON AND COLLEAGUES,** *Crucial Conversations*

First, figure out the scope of the conflict.

1. Step one is to recognize that you are in a conflict situation. Regardless of the type of conflict, the conversation needed is crucial, not just conversational.

2. Step two is to identify which conflict dynamic you are working through—is it dyadic, intragroup, or intergroup? That way, you can focus on the right people for the crucial conversation.

3. Step three is to determine whether the conflict is about the task, the process, or the relationship. Keep in mind that the answer to this question might be different for everyone involved.

Once you've determined the scope and focus of the conflict, follow these steps to apply the Crucial Conversations model to the conflict:

Start with the Heart. Have everyone involved share what they want and don't want. The authors of *Crucial Conversations* explain that "when you name the game, you can stop playing it. Make an honest effort to discover your motive—what you want. Once you call into question the shifting desires of your heart, you can make conscious choices to change them."[17] Key questions to ask yourself are:

1. What do I want for myself?

2. For others?

3. For the relationship?

4. How would I behave if that's what I wanted?

```
HOW SHOULD              WHAT DO I
I BEHAVE?                WANT
                        FOR MYSELF?

        ( START WITH )
        (  THE HEART )

WHAT DO I               WHAT DO I
WANT FOR                 WANT
THE RELATIONSHIP?       FOR OTHERS?
```

Learn to Look. Look out for signs of silence or violence that threaten safety, like any of the following behaviors:

- Avoiding
- Masking
- Withdrawing
- Controlling
- Labeling
- Attacking

If you see these threats, go back to the first step, Start with the Heart, and seek common ground.

Each Shares Their Path. Have people share their narrative, or their path, about the situation. What were the facts according to that person? What did they conclude? Essentially, each shares their leaps up the Ladder of Inference. As people share, look for signs of silence or violence and regain safety by focusing on mutual goals and showing that you have heard the person by paraphrasing what they said.

These are just a few techniques and a very brief look at the Crucial Conversations model. We encourage you to take a deeper look and add this vital skill to your tool kit.

A STEM METAPHOR TO DRIVE THE POINT HOME: PROBLEM DETECTION AND ROOT CAUSE ANALYSIS

Imagine that you designed a system that could never detect problems. It just runs and runs regardless of whether something has gone wrong. That's what it's like when a team can't distinguish between a casual conversation and a crucial one.

Now imagine a system that can detect problems. That's when technical professionals get to engage in problem-solving. One method of problem-solving is root cause analysis. There are many ways to get to the root cause of a problem; the five whys is one good example. You keep asking why until you can't anymore. That process is like the unearthing process in a crucial conversation. Rather than assuming everyone has the same why as yourself, you each investigate each other's motives and understanding of the situation until you re-establish common ground. From that common ground, you can craft a solution together.

A STORY IN ACTION

Over the past several months, the team members seemed to be working well with one another. As the timeline began to force them into making some critical decisions, Leila took the lead and started expressing her ideas at a team meeting. The conversation started productively but then quickly turned towards conflict. Then Malcolm voiced a completely different opinion on what the next steps should be, along with a lengthy, somewhat accusatory response to why Leila's ideas would not work. Rather than building on Leila's approach, Malcolm looked to poke holes and create doubt, with some valid points and some extreme points. The rest of the team found themselves either on Leila's side or Malcolm's side, except Joe.

The conversation channel became clogged because everyone was talking at the same time. There was no space to listen to any one person's input. Joe remained quiet as he listened to what he could decipher from the noise. He concluded he liked both ideas and could work with either option. It was also apparent to him that Malcolm and his side didn't trust Leila and her companions for some reason. The team had divided into two factions and had lost sight of the goal.

Soon the team turned their focus on Joe and his lack of participation. Michael, who sometimes ran a little high on emotions, accused Joe of not engaging. April stood up and started defending Joe, telling Michael that he was wrong. Leila politely interrupted the sidebar argument between April and Michael about Joe and asked, "What are we discussing?" Everyone looked around the room in silence.

Joe broke the silence and named the situation. He said that he had been observing rather than jumping into the debate, and he had noticed that the team was in a moment of conflict, which requires crucial conversation. Joe said, "I think something is going on with trust—it's not clear why we don't trust each other's ideas and incorporate both concepts. It appears that we've lost sight of our overall goal as a team. Can we go back to that?"

Malcolm took a deep breath and owned his part in being triggered by the opposition. He said that instead of sharing what was bothering him, he had kept pushing his point. He said, "I wasn't comfortable with Leila suddenly stepping up and taking charge, which is something I haven't seen her do in the past, and that made me anxious about her ideas. I have strong opinions of what I want, but I am open to figuring out what we think as a team." By voicing his experience, the team could shift into a crucial conversation to explore one another's concerns and fears and address the questions at hand.

REFLECTION QUESTIONS

- When you experience conflict, how do you respond?
- How can you start identifying the shift from casual to crucial conversations? Rather than jumping into debate, how can you cultivate your pause as Joe did?
- Do you believe all conflict is destructive? Have you seen instances where conflict ultimately lead to a better outcome? What can be the consequence of not addressing a conflict or sweeping it under the rug?
- What is a technique from the Crucial Conversations model that you'd especially like to focus on and try to practice more?

FURTHER READING AND REFERENCES

On the more casual side . . . a book to check out:

Patterson, Kerry, Joseph Grenny, Ron McMillan, and Al Switzler. (2012). *Crucial Conversations: Tools for Talking When Stakes Are High.*

On the more academic side . . . references we used:

Dyer, W. Gibb, Jr., Jeffrey H. Dyer, and William G. Dyer. (2013). *Team Building: Proven Strategies for Improving Team Performance.*

Jehn, K. A., and C. Bendersky, "Intragroup Conflict in Organizations: A Contingency Perspective on the Conflict-Outcome Relationship." *Research in Organizational Behavior.* https://doi.org/10.1016/S0191-3085(03)25005-X.

3.5

LEVERAGING DIVERSITY | POLARITY THINKING

Make sure that you are seeing each person on your team with fresh eyes every day. People evolve, and so your relationships must evolve with them. Care personally; don't put people in boxes and leave them there.

—**KIM MALONE SCOTT,** *Radical Candor*

THE PROBLEM These are just *some* of the challenges you might encounter that leveraging diversity using polarity thinking helps solve.	• Do you or your team members struggle to invite differences into your work together? • Do you often choose to go it alone or divide and conquer with team tasks rather than collectively leveraging wisdom? • Do you wonder how to bring together the different talents and strengths of you and your team members?

The saying goes, "If you want something done right, do it yourself," but is that realistic? Why do we need to work in teams? In the book *Team Building*, the authors explain that "the primary reason is that products and services have become increasingly complex, utilizing a wide range of skills and technologies. No single person is capable of developing, manufacturing, and selling today's increasingly complex products—which means that teams of individuals with *complementary* knowledge must coordinate effectively in order to be successful."[18] In our world and our complex work, we need teams of people—especially different people with complementary skill sets.

The phrase *brain trust* posits that two or more brains are better than one and that there's a hidden stored wealth inside those minds. Although working with multiple people can initially feel inefficient or just plain hard, the reality is that, ultimately, we get more done working together than we do by ourselves. However, this requires a shift in the typical scarcity mindset, which says that there is only enough space for one person to shine—and that it should be you.

Instead of thinking about competing for limited space, we can think of honoring the unique contributions that you and others make to a shared space—holding an abundant mindset that there is plenty of room for everyone. Some of us might already think that teamwork isn't a problem to be solved but a great way to get the work done. If you're already there, you might already be asking yourself, "How can we make the most of the strengths of all our team members?"

By exploring different perspectives and using appreciative thinking, we can appreciate the differences and the strengths that we have as individuals and that others have that we don't. This appreciation expands our thinking away from an either/or mentality, which tell us "either I do it, or it will not get done right." It moves us towards both/and thinking, which tell us "the team and I need to work on it, and it will be far better than any one person's idea." Here, we build on part 1's focus on the individual and individual strengths to think about how to identify and use individual strengths on a team.

LEVERAGING DIVERSITY THROUGH POLARITY THINKING

Here we share two ways to open up our eyes to the strengths we each might have and how we can make use of those strengths: polarity thinking and appreciative thinking. If you find that team members are often on opposing sides in discussions and it seems like the approaches are coming from different angles, polarity thinking can help. When it looks like the choices are either/or, polarity thinking prompts us to explore whether the option can be both/and.[19] Polarities represent a tension between two sides of an issue, but in reality, they are interdependent pairs with both truth and wisdom that need each other. Take, for example, breathing. Is inhaling or exhaling more critical? Well, both are equally important. If you had one without the other, you would not be living. The same is true with many positions we individually take. To us, they are the only right way. However, our view and the views of others all hold truth and wisdom and are inaccurate without one another.

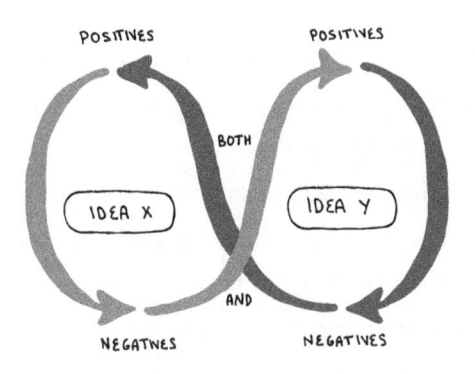

```
        POSITIVES           POSITIVES
              ↑                   ↑
            BOTH
      ( IDEA X )          ( IDEA Y )
              ↓                   ↓
                     AND
       NEGATIVES          NEGATIVES
```

Simply asking what aspects are valuable about our views can help break through either/or thinking. Often, other team members will see those valuable aspects before the presenter sees them. But it is vital as presenters of a point of view to leave room to change your perspective and be flexible. Sometimes we don't feel like we are being authentic unless we point out a problem or offer a critique of what still needs to be accomplished. Using polarity thinking, we can deliver our input with an and statement rather than a binary either/or, which will open the floodgates of innovation. In the book *Team Building*, the authors put it this way:

> When diversity is not managed effectively, differences can split people apart, cause endless arguments and bickering, and result in bitter feelings, resentment, and less productive work. When team members have obvious differences, one of their goals should be to achieve a level of constructive controversy. Used in this context, controversy is defined as the willingness to explore all sides of every issue. Achieving controversy is therefore a desired goal, not something to avoid.[20]

That is how you honor and receive the best output as a team, rather than relying on your knowledge and expertise of what you think is the best—remember you have a Blind window of things you don't know that you don't know!

There are also times when we are not in conflict or expressing opposite points of view on a team. Instead, we are just trying to organize the work effectively or brainstorm together as a team. In these situations, appreciative thinking can help make the most of team strengths.

In appreciative thinking, we are actively searching for what is exceptional and then figuring out how to make that the norm. Rather than looking at everything as a problem to solve, we can look for what is working well and figure out how to support and enhance that strength to drive even better outcomes. When things are not working, we ask what is working and choose to solve the problem by focusing on what is working well, rather than solving the issues that are not working. In this way, we become appreciative—we focus our energy on what we want to grow.

These concepts rely on the underlying belief that leveraging more minds is better than using only one brain on a problem. Pay attention to what makes others unique and how each person contributes positively to the team. Draw out others' knowledge, insight, and contribution by using Appreciative Inquiry to drive the conversation—notice the times when you show a rigid posture or attitude, when you come across as judgmental or dogmatic. Look for ways to articulate differences while managing any triggers that might come up for you or others. All of the topics in this part help form a culture where differences are more likely to be heard and appreciated.

PUTTING THE CONCEPT INTO PRACTICE

Polarities are maximizing the upside of the independent pair of ideas.

- **LOOK** for the polarity. What are two ideas that seem to be opposite each other?

- **MAP** out the best parts of both ideas.

- **ASSESS** the downsides of both ideas.

- **LEARN** the best parts of both to create more synergy and a better outcome.

- **LEVERAGE** those outcomes for the success of both ideas.

For appreciative thinking, try the following:

- Get clear on your strengths and the strengths of others on the team. Use assessments like the StrengthsFinder,[21] Tilt 365,[22] or other strength-based tests to drive the conversation and achieve clarity. Remember that strengths can change and shift over time, so be open to learning about new strengths with your colleagues and watch out for fixed mindsets.

- Have a dialogue on what helps each of you bring your strengths out. When are you at your best? What are you doing? What are others doing? What resources do you have in the environment?

- Now turn your attention to the team as a collective. What are your team's exceptional or stand-out strengths? When is your team at its most exceptional? How can you all support making that exception state the norm?

Once you have clarity as a team on the above questions, you can use the insights the next time you're assigning tasks, brainstorming solutions, or working together.

A STEM METAPHOR TO DRIVE THE POINT HOME: POTENTIAL ENERGY

One of the five forces in nature is potential energy. Imagine that every person you meet has potential energy—and it might be different from yours. As a team, you are trying to identify that potential energy and figure out ways to turn that into kinetic energy—action. How can you make it easy for that potential energy to transform? What is the analogy for creating a downhill path that is easy to roll down for a person? What is the team doing to make uphill paths people have to trudge up to bring out their strengths?

A STORY IN ACTION

Beth, a new supervisor, was eager to start her new position. She wanted to incorporate all the best practices of leadership she had experienced over the years. To show her credibility and value to the team, Beth had meetings every day, all day long, with her team. She wanted to show them how much she knew and cared about them.

While doing so, she found her team was less responsive to getting the work done on time. She started helping more and eventually took over where she thought the team needed help. As time soon showed, her team was unproductive, unresponsive, and showed low engagement.

Now working long hours, Beth needed a break one evening and walked out to the plant to get a fresh perspective. She observed a plant manager engage with his team. It impressed her, and she wondered what she was doing wrong with her team. As that week went by, Beth would walk out to the plant around the same time and observe the manager interacting with his team. After several observations, she finally asked him what his process was. He said to her, "I know the people who work for me, what they are good at, where they need help, and I get out of the way to let them do their job." He mentioned that each employee is different, but they all bring something that no other person brings to the team. Beth thought that was too simple and pressed him for more. He said, "That's all I have for you."

Beth reflected on what she was doing. She realized that she was spending too much time in meetings trying to impress her team by proving her technical and nontechnical skills. Because of all those meetings, the team members didn't have time to do their jobs and felt that more effort would not pay off. Beth shifted her approach and started learning each person's strengths, likes, and dislikes. She identified where they would need her help, and then she set them loose to get the work done. She shifted from thinking that she needed to do everything to thinking that the team can do everything. This shift fostered a better work environment for the team and a better work-life balance for Beth.

REFLECTION QUESTIONS

- What situations do you encounter where you feel you're the only one who can do the task?

- How can you best recruit others to be part of the task's success?

- What strengths do you bring to your team? What strengths do you appreciate about each of your team members?

- How can you combine the techniques from the topics on trust, psychological safety, navigating conflict, and polarity thinking to create an environment that drives diversity in your team?

FURTHER READING AND REFERENCES

On the more casual side . . . books and resources to check out:

Rath, T. (2007). *StrengthsFinder 2.0.*

Scott, Kim Malone. (2019). *Radical Candor.*

Tilt 365. (2022). "Strengths Assessment: You Are So Much More Than Your Personality." https://www.tilt365.com.

On the more academic side . . . references we used:

Dyer, W. Gibb, Jr., Jeffrey H. Dyer, and William G. Dyer. (2013). *Team Building: Proven Strategies for Improving Team Performance.*

Johnson, B. (1996). *Polarity Management: Identifying and Managing Unsolvable Problems.*

PART 4

$$N = \frac{X_1}{\sum_{i-n}^{n} X_i}$$

THE FIRST PRINCIPLES OF LEADING TEAMS

Authority is something that is built or created. It flows from many places to many people.

—**SMITH AND BERG,** *Paradoxes of Group Life*

There's often a moment when working on a team when you feel a leadership opportunity. It may be a formal assignment of leadership. But often, it is an informal, invisible force drawing you into a role of authority, even when not officially asked. In either situation, leading a team involves bringing individuals together, forming them into a team, and tracking progress towards a collective goal. In the context of informal authority, which often applies to technical professionals, additional considerations and capabilities can be needed to serve your team effectively.

In this part, we will highlight various ways to manage the significant shift from being an individual contributor to being an effective informal or formal team leader. In this part, we focus on project teamwork rather than people management (see part 5 for managing others).

Here are some of the most common situations in which the contents of this part might be applicable:

- **YOU ARE FORMALLY ASSIGNED AS TEAM OR PROJECT LEAD:** In this situation, everyone on the team is aware that you are the team lead due to a formal assignment from upper management or as the result of a team decision (in less hierarchical organizations). This includes having responsibility for part of a project or for a complete project timeline and scope.

- **YOU ARE GIVEN OR TAKE AUTHORITY INFORMALLY DURING A PROJECT:** In this situation, you may see a leadership opportunity. Perhaps the team is in a chaotic state, and you see a path forward. Or your subject matter expertise gives greater weight to your input.

- **YOU ARE PULLED IN AND OUT OF PROJECTS TO SERVE AS A SUBJECT EXPERT:** In this situation, you might not get to have as much influence on the project outcomes as you would like, but because you have unique technical expertise, you are asked for your time and your input (which may or may not be used).

- **YOU ARE INVOLVED IN A SPECIFIC PHASE OF A LONGER-TERM PROJECT:** You might be asked to step up and lead a specific phase of a project. In this situation, you might find yourself heavily involved in one or more stages of a project, depending on the type of project. Managing time and resources during these stages can be challenging but necessary to alleviate additional stress or pressure on you and your team.

To help you navigate these situations, this part includes the following topics:

- **LEADING VS DOING (PAGE 169):** You will learn the difference between an individual contributor, manager, and leader as we explore the concept of adaptive leadership.

- **STARTING UP A TEAM EFFORT (PAGE 181):** You will learn how to intentionally design a kickoff meeting and how to use other meetings as powerful momentum builders.

- **EFFECTIVELY USING AUTHORITY (PAGE 194):** You will learn about power dynamics—especially collaborative power.

- **MAKING DECISIONS TOGETHER (PAGE 203):** You will find different sensemaking and decision-making methods.

- **CELEBRATING TEAMWORK (PAGE 217):** You will learn how to celebrate and create closure for team milestones, slowdowns, and endings.

> **CONNECT BACK TO WHY**
>
> One of the greatest collaboration stories of our time has been the global pandemic of 2020 through 2022. As put in the magazine *Nature*, "The speed and scale of achievement during the pandemic is rare, if not unprecedented. Moreover, collaborating in the face of relentless media scrutiny as the world waited for a vaccine breakthrough has not been easy. Researchers need to study how this happened, in part to build on successes, and also to learn lessons for future pandemics, and to nurture the collaborations needed to tackle them."[1] Your ability to navigate collaboration can have world-changing consequences.

FURTHER READING AND REFERENCES

On the more academic side . . . references we used:

Editorial Board. (2021). "COVID Has Shown the Power of Science–Industry Collaboration." *Nature*. https://doi.org/10.1038/d41586-021-01580-0.

Smith, Kenwyn K., and David N. Berg. (1997). *Paradoxes of Group Life: Understanding Conflict, Paralysis, and Movement in Group Dynamics.*

4.1
LEADING VS. DOING | ADAPTIVE VS. TOXIC LEADERSHIP

Effective managers have to become skilled in the art of "reading" the situations that they are attempting to organize or manage. For this reason, it's often believed that effective managers have a kind of magical power to understand and transform the situations that they encounter. However, we find that this kind of mystique is often based on the ability to develop a deep appreciation of the situations being addressed.

—**GARETH MORGAN,** *Images of Organization*

THE PROBLEM These are just *some* of the challenges you might encounter that using adaptive leadership helps solve.	<ul><li>Do you struggle with letting go of doing the work and delegating to others?</li><li>Do you sense that your role focuses on tracking your team rather than empowering your team?</li><li>Are you interested in being a manager of a team that your team members don't want to leave?</li><li>Are you curious about the difference between good managers and great leaders?</li></ul>

In an ideal world, everyone on your team would execute their jobs flawlessly on their own. You'd never need to check up on their progress. Each team member would overcome his or her own challenges and work harmoniously with everyone around them. But that's not reality. The fact is, when people are working on team projects, people need regular input, guidance, and check-ins to stay effective and productive. Sometimes, people need these check-ins to hold them accountable for timely progress and to stay on track. Other times, it is helpful to have a regular opportunity to discuss current barriers to moving forward and how to work through them.

By definition, being a part of a larger team means the work cannot be done by one person alone. Coordinating and convening work is a task in itself. And, although it would be great to work well with everyone, challenges occur. And even when those conflicts are few, they must be addressed. Managers serve an essential function—they lead the team and coordinate all the team members' work to ensure progress towards a mutually shared vision. But not just any leader can do this. The best teams are led by a leader who supports the team members who are doing the work and who does not jump in and do the work themselves.

It's a big move from doing the work to leading others to do the work, whether you're formally assigned a leadership role or not. We're so accustomed to doing our work as an individual contributor that it can be hard and time-consuming to delegate things we can do easily. It feels like it would take less time if we just did it ourselves. And although we might have excellent technical skills, we might be uncertain about our people management skills—that task can feel ill-defined and ambiguous.

Further complicating the task of people management is that the difference between a manager and a leader is a source of great discussions and debates. The late Warren Bennis delineated the two like this: A manager is one who plans, organizes, and coordinates, and a leader is one who inspires and motivates.[2] Although they are two different skill sets, you can't have an outstanding leader without good managerial skills any more than you can have a skilled manager without good leadership skills.

Sometimes managerial responsibilities are referred to as soft skills. However, these skills are anything but easy. They are difficult to master because of all the issues covered in the previous parts—we humans are complex individuals, and complexity grows as we layer, integrate, and coordinate together. With the rise of workers whose talent is centered on contributing knowledge[3] (known as knowledge workers) rather than routine skills, there is less need for managing people for efficiency's sake. Instead, the task is to lead people by tapping into every individual contributor's specialized knowledge and skills to empower innovation. When you step into a leadership role, it's important to avoid falling into the trap of becoming a micromanager or a toxic leader who controls others. Instead, focus on becoming an *adaptive leader*. This approach to leadership will allow you to retain your team members' respect and commitment and help you develop an effective team.

LEADING VS. DOING THROUGH ADAPTIVE VS. TOXIC LEADERSHIP BEHAVIORS

Management is doing things right; leadership is doing the right things.

—PETER DRUCKER, *The Effective Executive*

All leaders were once individual contributors. As an individual contributor, you were probably great at the technical aspect of your job. You stayed well connected to the industry trends and could use the latest tools and techniques to push past obstacles. At some point, your technical prowess caught the attention of others, and you were promoted. Rising in the organizational hierarchy is a common professional goal, and we often get hooked on winning new titles and promotions. You might have really enjoyed your work as an individual contributor, and you may have taken a promotion without fully realizing that it would involve a change from doing the technical work to leading others to do that very work you had enjoyed doing yourself.

Now, as a leader of individual contributors, your challenge is to create the same passion you once had for the technical work in others who are now taking on the job that used to be yours. You have to focus less on the technical work itself and more on the people. You need to foster an environment of trust and employee involvement and be mindful of differing viewpoints—yours and others'. Naturally, you will become less connected to the latest tools and techniques, which will cause you to rely on others to provide good information to make decisions. And, lastly, your responsibility has grown from a focus on your own tasks to a focus on empowering everyone on the team to deliver their best work.

The speed at which you have to step up and take on these responsibilities might feel overwhelming at times, especially because of the demand to meet customers' needs. With these pressures in your new role, you might default to the easiest—and often worst—responses. You might be even more prone than usual to climb up the Ladder of Inference. You might react in response to the Four Fatal Fears or be too biased in your decision-making. We have all been exposed to toxic bosses. We learn what not to do versus what to do most of the time by observing their behaviors. Toxic bosses have been shown to produce counterproductive working behaviors in their teams, create undue psychological distress and depression, reduce job satisfaction, and increase workplace bullying.

One way to spot toxic bosses is to observe whether they micromanage the team or the product. Unlike a new manager who might be a little more hands on than you like, a micromanager's intense interference stifles the productivity and performance of the team. New managers who don't learn to trust the team members and let them do the work will find themselves micromanaging as a result. The interesting thing is that no manager aspires to be a micromanager. It just happens over time because, for any number of reasons, they feel more comfortable doing the work than learning how to lead others to do the work.

As mentioned, management and leadership are two different skill sets that complement each other. Managers are considered specialists in their discipline. Someone who manages has navigated through similar projects in the past and helps the team focus on tracking and solving issues with time, schedule, and resources. Here are some examples of the kinds of questions a manager typically asks:

- Are we on track to meet our next milestone? If we are off schedule, to what extent are we off and why?

- Are we on or off budget? If we are off, to what extent are we off and why?

- Who or what is keeping us from meeting our timeline or budget?

A leader, on the other hand, becomes more of a generalist. A generalist is someone who focuses on resolving the team members' needs, barriers, and concerns and fosters their strengths, interconnections, and relationships. The focus is less on fixing the problem and more on helping the team members anticipate and define the problems they are trying to solve. Here are some examples of the kinds of questions a leader asks:

- What do my team members need to do their best?

- What market trends should we be paying attention to?

- How would we respond to different types of disruptors in our market?

Management and leadership skills can be best understood through a leadership framework called *adaptive leadership*.[4] Adaptive leadership involves activities that mobilize, motivate, organize, orient, and focus attention on addressing and tackling tough challenges while still thriving. The main metaphor used in adaptive leadership is the dance floor and the balcony. As put by Ronald Heifetz and colleagues in their book *The Practice of Adaptive Leadership*, "To diagnose a system or yourself while in the midst of action requires the ability to achieve some distance from those on-the-ground events. We use the metaphor of 'getting on the balcony' above the 'dance floor' to depict what it means to gain the distanced perspective you need to see what is really happening."[5] The dance floor is where management takes place. Many things in business require management skills to create order out of chaos. While those management skills are essential, they can limit one's view. It can be hard to see the reality of the challenges when in the thick of the situation.

Moving to the balcony provides a different vantage point. This is where leadership takes place. The perspective from the balcony momentarily offers managers time to step back from the situation's noise, activities, and chaos to see the big picture and a clearer view of reality. This space for observation offers leaders the bandwidth to think of ways to inspire and motivate. Although while on the balcony a leader is temporarily removed from the challenge, it doesn't mean they are disconnected from what is happening on the dance floor. In fact, effective managers and leaders can move back and forth between the dance floor (management) to the balcony (leadership) throughout the day. In the "Putting the Concept into Practice" section below, we share more about how to build adaptive leadership skills.

PUTTING THE CONCEPT INTO PRACTICE

Your goal should be to keep the temperature within what we call the productive zone of disequilibrium (PZD): enough heat generated by your intervention to gain attention, engagement, and forward motion, but not so much that the organization (or your part of it) explodes.

—**RONALD A. HEIFETZ AND COLLEAGUES,** *The Practice of Adaptive Leadership*

To increase your ability to move back and forth from the dance floor and the balcony, here are the 4 As of adaptive leadership. By understanding the 4 As, you minimize the time and effort it takes to switch your thought processes from the balcony to the dance floor and vice versa.

- **ANTICIPATION** of the future needs, trends, and opportunities (balcony).
    - Business is full of the unknown unknowns; however,

**ANTICIPATION
ACCOUNTABILITY**

**ADAPTABLE
ARTICULATION**

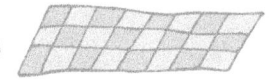

paying particular attention to the political, economic, and environmental landscape surrounding your industry helps give you the foresight to see big shifts coming your way.

- **ARTICULATION** of what these challenges might look like for the team and potential options for handling them (dance floor).

  - Change is a constant variable in the world. The team can discover hypothetical solutions to potential big shifts that might hinder their productivity through scenario planning.

- **ADAPTATION** to each challenge by creating a safe atmosphere to tackle difficult problems one at a time (dance floor).

  - People aren't necessarily opposed to change itself, but they may be opposed to the way the change is being imposed on them. Creating psychological safety (topic 3.3) to express concerns and oppositions will expedite their openness to a new process and foster a new level of comfort with change.

- **ACCOUNTABILITY** to give the work back to the team members while providing some direction and structure (balcony).

  - Leaders can get their teams to be either compliant or

committed. When team members are empowered and given the discretion to get the job done, they will be committed and will rise to the occasion. If you tell them what and how to get it done, they might be compliant, but that will require more work to hold them accountable than one has time for.

A STEM METAPHOR TO DRIVE THE POINT HOME: CONTEXT SWITCHING

Context switching is a concept that originated in computer science. The idea involves storing the current state of a process or context so that it can be restored and reloaded quickly, which allows the process to resume execution more quickly. In human behavior terms, it's similar to multitasking or task switching. Although, in theory, switching is thought of as getting multiple tasks done simultaneously, it is a time sucker because of the cognitive start-up required to switch from one task to the next. However, the more closely related the skills or tasks are to one another, the less cognitive effort is required to switch. This is analogous to building skills for leading versus doing. One switch you could make is between doing or leading. However, you will be even more efficient if you stick to switching between understanding what's happening on the dance floor (rather than doing) versus leading from the balcony.

A STORY IN ACTION

Edgar has led the product development team for the past twelve months. He has been effective at being on time, on budget, and on specification. His team is highly skilled and agile. Throughout various projects, Edgar would come up with new ideas that created more work for the team and were seldom implemented. The team members shared with Edgar their frustration about his out-of-scope ideas and the challenges they created for the project.

One of the team members, Jasmine, is leaving the company. Her role is very important and highly technical. Several team members asked about taking over some of her responsibilities. They had the skills to do her tasks but would need to take unnecessary items off their plate—including Edgar's spontaneous new ideas.

Instead of giving others the chance to step up, Edgar decided he would take on Jasmine's responsibilities while searching for an outside candidate to fill her role. The search has taken much longer than expected. After a few months in which Edgar continued to do Jasmine's work, the project has suffered.

The team is no longer on time, on budget, or on specification. The team failed to deliver on specific tasks and deliverables. The team felt Edgar didn't trust them to do the job, and instead of delegating the work, he took it over and did it himself.

After a long week, Edgar was still at the office, exhausted, while everyone else had left for the weekend. Taking a break from looking at his computer, he realized he had made a rookie mistake by taking on Jasmine's responsibilities instead of inspiring and supporting others to step up.

REFLECTION QUESTIONS

- How much of your time is spent planning, organizing, and coordinating versus inspiring and motivating?

- How often do you step in and take over when things don't look the way you think they should?

FURTHER READING AND REFERENCES

On the more casual side . . . a resource to check out:

> Next Generation. (2002). "The Difference Between Leadership and Management." https://www.nextgeneration.ie/blog/2018/03/the-difference-between-leadership-and-management.

On the more academic side . . . references we used:

> Bennis, Warren G. (1989). *On Becoming a Leader.*
>
> Drucker, Peter. (2006). *The Effective Executive.*
>
> Heifetz, Ronald A., Marty Linsky, and Alexander Grashow. (2009). *The Practice of Adaptive Leadership: Tools and Tactics for Changing Your Organization and the World.*
>
> Morgan, Gareth. (2006). *Images of Organizations.*

4.2

STARTING UP A TEAM EFFORT | DESIGNING THE KICKOFF AND OTHER MEETINGS

Start strong, stay strong, and finish strong by always remembering why you're doing it in the first place.

—**RALPH MARSTON,** *The Daily Motivator*

THE PROBLEM These are just *some* of the challenges you might encounter that intentionally designing the kickoff and meetings helps solve.	• Do you get easily frustrated when a team first starts and isn't instantly productive? • Do you struggle with how to jumpstart a team or get it unstuck? • Do you know where to begin with a new team? • Do you find that new team members hold back the team's progress?

It happened overnight. You made the shift from one of us to one of them. That's how it might sometimes feel when you go from being an equal team member to being the team lead, a position naturally perceived as more elevated. Although nothing physically changed, the dynamics of the relationships changed and perceptions changed. One of the many challenges in taking on a leadership role is overcoming the perception of leaders as villains.

Leading a healthy team formation process that supports equal contributions and leads to exceptional output helps convert the "us and them" attitude to a "we" mentality. The we mentality looks at what motivates individuals and teams to get the work started and helps us finish the work with the same drive. Leveraging the different expertise and personal strengths of team members helps shape the team's collective wisdom into a strong bond.

The initial start of a team can be messy. The proverbial "So now what do we do?" question can take days—and sometimes weeks—to sort through and get moving. Often team members have overlapping expertise and strengths, and this overlap can create conflict in some areas and a lack of certain expertise and strength in other areas. As the leader of the team and the person driving its formation, you're forced to step back and examine how each individual can contribute so that collectively you can accomplish what no single person can do alone.

This is where the concept of team formation can be extremely helpful. From part 3, we already know that teams develop over time. Using Tuckman's model, we shared that the first stage of team development is forming. We know that one way or another, the team will come together and form their work process, roles, and norms. But rather than using a haphazard approach, what strategies could you use to intentionally and efficiently navigate the formation stage?

Believe it or not, it is possible for a team to produce positive, productive work within a few hours or within the first meeting or two, rather than taking weeks to build momentum! When you are formally assigned as a team leader, it is easier to speak up and start organizing everyone. When you're on a team where no lead has been clearly identified, the ideas shared in this topic may help you start guiding the team, albeit from a more informal standpoint. The key concept is to intentionally and formally design a team kickoff meeting.

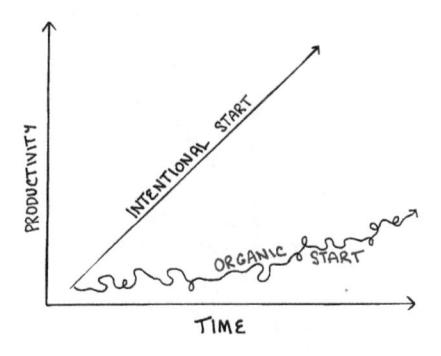

STARTING UP A TEAM BY DESIGNING THE KICKOFF MEETING AND OTHER MEETINGS

Some days, many of us feel like we go from one meeting to the next. There is little time for actual work to be done because we are in meetings talking about the work that needs to be done. In a meeting, you might think to yourself, "Why am I in this meeting?" Time is a nonrenewable resource that we all treasure but seldom protect. It is estimated that 37 percent of the time spent in meetings adds no value to the work.[6] The reason for these unproductive meetings is the lack of an established purpose or agenda for the meeting. Everyone shows up, but no one knows exactly why they are there that day.

UNINTENTIONAL PATH OF TEAM START UP

INTENTIONAL PATH OF TEAM START UP

One of the most impactful yet undervalued skills in our day-to-day lives at work is meeting design. And the design of a kickoff meeting is particularly important. If leaders don't take the time to intentionally design a kickoff meeting at the start of a project, the team may simply muddle through and self-organize inefficiently. Intentional, well-designed team kickoff meetings serve the following purposes.

- **TEAM BUILDING:** Good team kickoffs give this new team (or an old team on a new project) a chance to get to know one another and build (or renew) trust.

- **ESTABLISH EXPECTATIONS:** Good team kickoffs develop team charters together and become aligned on the scope of work, team member responsibilities, team norms, timelines, and success criteria.

- **WALK THROUGH LOGISTICS AND SYSTEMS:** The often dry task of logistics gets taken care of in the kickoff. How will the project be managed, including meeting frequency and task management tracking?

- **FIRST WINS:** Initial next steps are discussed as well as immediate next action items. Strong kickoffs make sure these next steps are also immediate wins for the team and feel like momentum-building progress.

Dialogue is an essential component of kickoff meetings. The kickoff meeting leads to greater team effectiveness when leaders create space for the team to discuss and arrive at conclusions related to the above purposes. Alternatively, when leaders come to the team kickoff with all the answers and plans already established, they find the team feels shut down and acts more as order takers than engaged contributors to the project.

The team charter, shared in part 3, is a primary tool and deliverable for the team kickoff. Recall that a team charter is a document that outlines the purpose, the scope, the team members and team norms, and measured results. Its primary goal is to set and manage expectations. A team charter defines the work we do (and don't do), who is assigned to which part of the work (responsibilities), and how the work gets done (process). It helps us discover all the moving parts, resources, and external partners needed to get the work done. Chartering expectations and responsibilities shows the interconnection and importance of everyone's roles based on their strengths and other parameters.

By putting expectations down on paper, where everyone can see, align, and discuss them, a leader mitigates the "us versus them" and "me, myself, and I" mindsets and encourages a we mentality instead. As a leader, you may fill in some of the blanks of a team charter initially and leave others open for the team members to discuss and arrive at the answers together. Team charters can be used in the kickoff as well as throughout the team's work. Consider the following ways a team charter can be used.

- **AS AN ORGANIZING MECHANISM FOR THE TEAM'S FIRST MEETINGS:** The categories of a team charter can easily be used to create the agenda for initial meetings and to create questions that the team members can discuss together.

- **AS A TOOL TO DRIVE TEAM DISCUSSION:** While a leader (assigned or otherwise) might have some ideas of how to fill in the blanks, the team members should all participate and contribute ideas and ultimately become aligned to what is captured in the kickoff meeting.

- **AS AN ANCHOR TO RETURN TO OVER AND OVER:** A good team charter defines the work the team will do, but it also captures what the team does not do. It helps clarify who is assigned to which part of the work (responsibilities) and how the work gets done (process).

- **AS A LIVING DOCUMENT:** While it serves as an anchor, that anchor should not be seen as fixed in stone but rather as resting in the sand. If the scope, responsibilities, or process need to be shifted, returning to the charter and revising it is a key activity to maintain team health.

In the "Putting the Concept into Practice" section, we provide general guidelines for meeting design.

PUTTING THE CONCEPT INTO PRACTICE

For kickoff meetings and meetings in general, facilitating and structuring efficient meetings is a valuable skill. Before a meeting happens, if it's not clear already, it's helpful to identify who will be leading or facilitating the meeting. It is generally the responsibility of the person hosting the meeting. Facilitating good meetings not only produces good outcomes that create more productivity but also brings people together for good morale. But often, meetings get overly complex. Here are some of the main factors to consider for good meeting design, whether you're meeting in person or virtually.

- **HAVE A CLEAR PURPOSE AND CHOOSE THE TYPE OF MEETING:** Are you gathering to share information? Make a decision? Brainstorm? Engage in a working session? Check in? Team building? Post-project debrief? Sharing security or critical mission communication? The purpose and type of meeting drive the agenda, length, prework, and more.

- **WHO IS INVOLVED IN THE MEETING:** Sometimes we want to include everyone in the meeting just to keep them up to date. But there are other, more efficient, ways to keep people informed, as we have already discussed. Determining all of the key people who need to attend is only one step. Attendees should be informed about why they are expected to attend and what is expected of them at the meeting. This will help people prepare, but this step is also helpful when determining whether they need to attend.

- **DEFINE PREWORK:** To help individuals, the team, and the organization succeed, you can implement short, effective ways to share and receive information with the team. With digital tools today, a lot can happen before or in place of a meeting. An example is through team collaboration software like Slack, Teams, Yammer, and other channels. Slack channels are organized conversations that bring order and clarity to work. Along with cloud collaboration tools like Google Drive, OneDrive, and other applications, this software allows your team members to think through, reflect, and share ideas at their own time and pace. This can actually help create more inclusive and thoughtful discussion for your team. People who speak less often in person might be more comfortable speaking up online. Brainstorming about project issues that require time to think can sometimes be done more effectively online than in a single meeting. You can choose from a variety of software or select the one that already exists at your organization. If it's not working for the team, choose another version that everyone has access to. With the right team norms about how to use the channel, teams can share ideas, make decisions, and move work forward.

- **CREATE AN AGENDA:** Meetings that are structured well are simple. There's a clear set of desired outcomes for the meeting and an idea of what will get the team to those outcomes. Having efficient but straightforward meetings makes it easy for people to collaborate. A great way to construct an agenda is to determine the questions that need to be answered. For each question, take time to articulate exactly what is needed or might generate the most helpful discussion. Then, determine the time each question might take or should take before moving on to the next item. The collaboration fosters information and knowledge sharing and is a terrific way to help everyone feel like part of the process. But not all collaboration has to be done in a long meeting.

- **DECIDE ON THE LENGTH OF THE MEETING:** The meeting should have a clear agenda that will help determine how long it would take to sufficiently exchange ideas, build a discussion about the ideas, vet out any decisions, and adequately assign who is responsible for what. For the sake of productivity and based on the level of complexity of the ideas to be discussed, there might need to be a series of meetings with clear agendas to provide time for data collection or collect other vital information that needs to be presented before reaching a decision.

- **SHORT MEETINGS CAN BE JUST AS, IF NOT MORE EFFECTIVE, AS LONG MEETINGS:** Business objectives are constantly changing, and teams are asked to produce more output with fewer resources. Therefore, time shouldn't be wasted on nonessential interactions. To help individuals, the team, and the organization succeed, you can implement short, effective ways to share and receive information with the team members.

- **CONSIDER ALTERNATIVES TO MEETINGS:** Depending on the purpose and desired outcomes of collaboration, you may consider whether one-on-one calls or smaller work groups, such as in trios or in breakout rooms, are a better fit than an entire team meeting. Another way is through huddles. Huddles, similar to daily stand-up, daily scrum, or sprint planning meetings, can be done virtually or face to face. They are short daily meetings (no more than fifteen minutes) for the entire team to get informed and aligned with others on the work that needs to be done. An effective huddle depends on everyone adhering to the team norm about what is shared and not shared during the huddles.

One sign that content is not worthy of being discussed in a meeting is if no one is asking a question after five to ten minutes of talking about that topic. If no one has questions, then in the future, you might want to use other methods of information sharing, like a Slack channel, email, or a physical or virtual flyer. This respects other people's time.

Along with the team charter, activities to build team trust are also a good idea. There are many tools and courses out there to help facilitators and hosts construct simple, engaging, efficient ways to host a meeting.

A STEM METAPHOR TO DRIVE THE POINT HOME: THE GENERAL LAW OF FRICTION

The general law of friction states that when one surface slides over another, the moving surface experiences a resisting force (aka friction force) against the direction in which it slides. The rougher the surfaces, the more significant the friction. In general, having either friction or no friction can serve a purpose. Friction provides the proper force so a car can move controllably on the road. No friction allows a process or movement to accelerate because there is no resistance. One way to control the amount of friction is to use a lubricant. The purpose of a lubricant is to fill the gap between the two surfaces, so they come together but are not in direct contact, thus reducing the amount of friction. The more lubricant, the less friction, and the less lubricant, the more the surfaces come in contact to create friction.

A STORY IN ACTION

Jimmy was selected to lead a new improvement initiative for an existing project. This is his first formal team lead role. Being new to this role, he was excited but apprehensive because he had mostly worked for leaders who taught him what not to do more than what to do. He wanted to start off by setting the team up for success by avoiding some of the conflicts he had seen in the past when expectations were unclear and people lacked clarity about their individual roles on the team.

He decided to use the team charter as a tool to kick off the team's work. After learning the expectations for the team purpose, success metrics, and project scope, Jimmy started outlining the team charter topics. As a first pass, he sketched out the key roles, skill sets, and support the team members would need to succeed. Then he realized the team needed more bandwidth to do their best work. He decided to bring on a few new team members to support the team and the project. With the help of his leadership and human resources, Jimmy crafted a job description and began recruiting a few more team members. After much time, he was finally able to assemble a full team.

At their official team kickoff, Jimmy introduced the concept of a team charter. Over the course of two meetings, he shared his plan that covered critical questions. He stated that his ideas were a starting point for discussion, and he looked forward to everyone's insights. Through asking a few thoughtful questions and leaving the remaining time open for dialogue and listening, the team built on the initial starting point to finalize the team charter.

As a result, everyone felt like they understood the project, their role, and the timeline. The team members felt excited and aligned with Jimmy's plan. Over the course of the project, each time a new team member was added, the project changed, or confusion arose, Jimmy and the team updated the charter so that everyone felt like a valuable part of the team.

REFLECTION QUESTIONS

- Have you ever experienced a time when you didn't know what you were responsible for versus what other team members were responsible for? Or when the work process or goals were unclear? What were some of the pros and cons of that experience?

- Have you participated or led a team charter process before kicking off a team's work? What was the experience like? What did you like about it? What would you change?

- Does your team have a team charter?

- How often is the charter reviewed to make sure it is still applicable?

- How have team norms helped or hindered your team from working together effectively?

- What changes to your team charter need to be made based on shifting priorities or expectations?

- How efficient are you with your time?

- Are you attending meetings you don't need to?

- How efficient are you with other people's time when you host a meeting?

- What's a recent meeting you enjoyed going to? What did you learn from the design of that meeting that you would like to try out?

- Does your team typically have a meeting lead assigned? What are the pros and cons of this approach for your team culture?

FURTHER READING AND REFERENCES

On the more casual side . . . books and resources to check out:

Marston, Ralph. (2002). *The Daily Motivator*. https://greatday.com/motivate/020628.html.

Mørch, Allan. (2017). "[Infographic] A One Hour Meeting Is Never Just a One Hour Meeting." https://www.askcody.com/blog/infographic-a-one-hour-meeting-is-never-just-a-one-hour-meeting.

Hyper Island Toolbox. https://toolbox.hyperisland.com.

Essential Meeting Facilitation Toolkit. https://www.sessionlab.com/meeting-facilitation-toolkit.

4.3
EFFECTIVELY USING AUTHORITY | COLLABORATIVE POWER

Taking the power that is available and using it often creates a vacuum because it is experienced as depriving others of a scarce commodity. As a result, power taking is resisted. On the other hand, if one takes the available power and uses it to empower others, the total amount of group and individual power increases.

— **SMITH AND BERG,** *Paradoxes of Group Life*

THE PROBLEM These are just *some* of the challenges you might encounter that using collaborative power helps solve.	• Do you struggle to get people to follow your lead? • Do you have informal authority rather than formal authority? • Do you struggle to get buy-in to your vision?

Once we are given or take the lead, we often think that people will automatically start to listen to our directions. Instead, we might find an undercurrent of resistance. Maybe some team members don't immediately believe you are credible. Perhaps some don't fully trust the direction and ideas you bring forward. Still others might feel they would do a better job leading or have personal experiences with you that create doubt or negativity.

One of the most challenging tasks for a leader is to feel comfortable with and effectively use their authority to move a team forward. Some leaders struggle with telling others what to do. Others find the same task too easy! They might dominate individual perspectives and not provide enough space for collaboration. At the core of these challenges is power.

Power dynamics refers to the ways in which power is at work in a situation. Your ability to understand the kind of power dynamics typically used in leadership situations is crucial. Your understanding of the power you hold and how you would like to use it influences the level of inclusivity, psychological safety, motivation, engagement, trust, and many other positive emotions experienced by your team members and direct reports. As psychologist Rollo May says about power, "Both [power and love] are conjunctive processes of being—a reaching out to influence others, molding, forming, creating the consciousness of the other. But this is only possible, in an inner sense, if one opens oneself at the same time to the influence of the other."[7]

In this topic, we introduce several ways of thinking about power, with a focus on collaborative power dynamics.

EFFECTIVELY USING AUTHORITY THROUGH COLLABORATIVE POWER

A huge obstacle in creating psychological safety, employee engagement, and positive culture are the dynamics of power, the use of it, and (sometimes) the abuse of power. Power refers to the functions of dependency and control. When a person or system has the ability to influence, control, or otherwise change our situation, they have the ability to exert power over us. And this can create a sense of dependency. The more dependent we are on people, systems, or beliefs, the more influence and power they have over us.

Power is not inherently wrong as long as it is used for the benefit of oneself and others. When you are new to a position of power, whether you have been formally given the role or informally taken on the leadership role, the way you use power can create resistance or create followership.

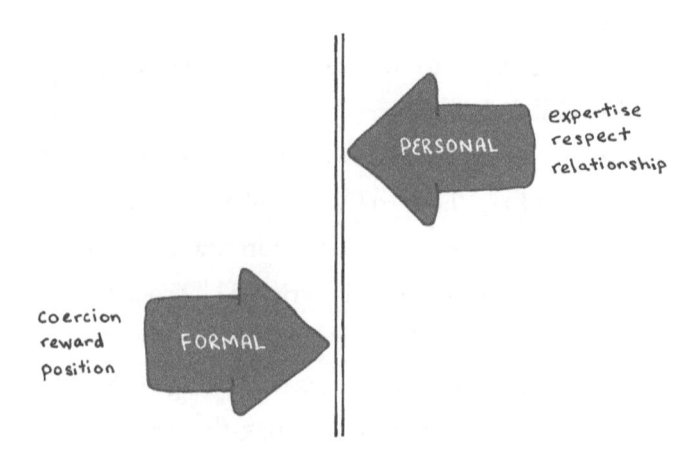

PERSONAL — expertise, respect, relationship

FORMAL — coercion, reward, position

There are two basic power structures: (1) formal and (2) personal.[8] The formal includes coercion (using fear), reward (this for that), and position (title). Formal power is commonly referred to as *power over* because it's expressed as a dominating force and activity and is primarily motivated by using fear and position to get what one wants or thinks is right. Power over is operating under the pretense that power is a finite resource, where some people should have it and others should not. Dominant voices use their power over others to diminish psychological safety—they don't leave space for alternative perspectives or being. In the book *Power and Love*, Adam Kahane puts it like this: "The degenerative, shadow side is power-over—the stealing or suppression of the self-realization of another."[9]

The second is personal, where one's expertise and respect can influence a situation for someone else. The personal form of power is more effective because it's rooted in a relationship instead of in positional power and authority. In relationships, we choose whether to engage or not and at what level to accept influence. To better understand personal power, we will look at three types of power: the power within, power with, and power to.[10]

POWER WITHIN

POWER WITH

POWER TO

The power within is at the heart of psychological safety. We first have to feel psychologically safe in who we are before we can extend psychological safety to others. To feel the power within is to give ourself permission and have the courage to take up space. It is the self-worth and belief that each of us matters and we belong, regardless of what other stories exist. It's unleashing our full potential and vulnerability to let others get to know us, and for us to get to know them (see part 1). In other words, we can't blame others for making us not feel safe to share when we ourselves struggle with vulnerability, confidence, and self-esteem and have not addressed those struggles.

Power with takes a collaborative approach to create psychological safety and is a team action. It forges a path to mutual respect and support for the benefit of everyone's success. It values the diversity of ideas, inclusiveness, and participation. Power with views information sharing as a competitive advantage since it encourages collective wisdom and action. Amy Edmondson describes a tactic for creating power within in her *Disrupt Yourself* podcast: "Questions are really powerful in creating safety—they indicate to someone that you actually want to hear their voice."[11] Most of our tips in the "Putting the Concept into Practice" section are about how to create power with environments rather than power over.

The *power to* approach creates psychological safety by empowering others. Adam Kahane explains that "when I am exercising my power-to, and I feel myself bumping up against you exercising yours [power-to], and if in this conflict, I have the capacity to prevail over you, then I can easily turn to exercise power over you."[12] Positive thinking about ourselves and others leads to a willingness to take some risks and share our authentic selves (see Johari Window, part 1). As a by-product of positive self-esteem, you create that same opportunity for your team. The power to is the power to make a difference and take responsibility for your ability to shine. And no one can take that away from you but you.

PUTTING THE CONCEPT INTO PRACTICE

Try applying these questions to a current situation: Right now, do you have the power to do something? Do you have power over something? Power with another? Are you using your power within?

To create healthier power dynamics, here are some places to start.

1. **LOOK OUT FOR POWER OVER SITUATIONS:** These situations often happen when there is a limited resource—whoever owns that resource will naturally have a dominating force. Whether that is who owns the budget, who assigns staffing resources, who makes decisions, or who takes notes on a call, these resources are not shared evenly across a team. At the least, being aware that these are limited resources can be helpful. In some cases, such as note-taking, the power of capturing everyone's voices accurately can become a shared, collaborative power dynamic by rotating the responsibility.

2. **MAKE SPACE FOR ALTERNATIVE PERSPECTIVES:** Share your views with confidence and provide supporting evidence but leave room at the end for reactions and differences.

3. **BEGIN BY PREFACING YOUR COMMENTS WITH PHRASES THAT SHOW YOU ARE FLEXIBLE:** Use phrases like "This is what I'm thinking so far, but it's not set in stone, and I'm open to changes."

4. **END WITH QUESTIONS TO HELP CONVERSATIONS FEEL LESS CLOSED OFF:** What do you all think about this? Does it resonate with your experience? What am I missing? What else would you add? Do you see it differently?

5. **WATCH OUT FOR TWO CRITICAL PIECES, PERFECTIONISM AND SILENCE:** These indicate a presence of power over in the room.

6. **WHEN THERE IS SILENCE, THERE IS LIKELY HIDING OF SELF HAPPENING IN THE ROOM:** If you are the speaker, it's worth shifting from statements to questions to invite engagement and open yourself up to judgment. If you are not the speaker, take a risk and ask what others are thinking.

7. **WHEN THERE IS A HIGH LEVEL OF CRITICISM, THERE'S A FOCUS ON PERFECTIONISM GOING ON:** But perfect is defined differently for each person. Criticism often stems from someone's idea of a standard. Instead of criticizing, it is best to go back and review what the standard is. Did a mistake really occur? And even if it did, are we expecting perfection from one another? Is it not about a mistake but a point of view someone strongly believes in? And when faced with an alternative viewpoint, is another person made to feel wrong? Are we as a team making space for more than one way to exist?

A STEM METAPHOR TO DRIVE THE POINT HOME: VECTOR QUANTITIES

Vector quantities are about both magnitude and direction. When comparing vectors, $A = B$ if the magnitude and the direction are the same. Otherwise, you could have vectors with the same direction but different magnitudes or vectors with the same magnitude but different directions. When vectors have the same magnitude and opposite directions, you have a negative vector. This is analogous to a power play, in which two people have equal power but act in opposite, conflicting directions. This also happens when a leader has a direction that a team opposes, either directly or passively. In that case, one vector is negative to the other. When you add two such vectors, they cancel each other out, and their sum equals a zero vector. Thus, the zero vector results in no magnitude and no direction.

REFLECTION QUESTIONS

- Can you recall an experience when you were at the receiving end of an unhealthy power dynamic? How did it feel? What was your reaction?

- Have you worked on growing your power within? Do you feel confident in your own views and taking up space with others? Or is it easy to feel your views are not as good as others?

- What power plays are in motion with your team?

- How does your behavior show power within, with, to, and over? Do you tend towards one power dynamic more than others?

FURTHER READING AND REFERENCES

On the more casual side . . . books and resources to check out:

Edmondson, Amy. (2019). "Psychological Safety." https://whitneyjohnson.com/amy-edmondson.

Kahane, Adam. (2009). "Beyond War and Peace." https://reospartners.com/an-introduction-to-power-and-love-a-theory-and-practice-of-social-change.

On the more academic side . . . references we used:

Kahane, Adam. (2009). *Power and Love: A Theory and Practice of Social Change.*

Smith, Kenwyn K., and David N. Berg. (1997). *Paradoxes of Group Life: Understanding Conflict, Paralysis, and Movement in Group Dynamics.*

4.4

MAKING DECISIONS TOGETHER | SENSEMAKING AND DECISION-MAKING METHODS

If you're not confused, you're not paying attention.

—**TOM PETERS,** *Thriving on Chaos*

THE PROBLEM These are just *some* of the challenges you might encounter that using sensemaking helps solve.	• Do you feel under pressure to make the best decisions on your own? • Do you feel overwhelmed by the complexity of what needs to be considered before making decisions? • Do you feel you've captured the team's wisdom during decision-making processes? • Do you think decisions tend to be biased or represent only a few dominant perspectives?

One aspect of a team leader's job is to arrive at the final decision through some process. Research has suggested that one nonnegotiable skill leaders must be good at is making decisions.[13] But what does it mean to make excellent decisions? When making decisions, there is a high probability that you will not please everyone. For example, the company might require you to lay off employees or stop working with particular vendors. While it might benefit the company, it clearly won't help the employees or vendors. Or your team may work together to weigh the pros and cons of potential solutions and decide on a solution, but aspects of the answer may not resonate well with particular team members. Or your team members might submit three different proposals on ways to move a project forward, and ultimately you can choose only one. The team member who produced the selected proposal will think you made a great decision, while the others may disagree.

Sometimes, when faced with a decision of the unknowns, as we've learned in earlier parts, we rely on experiences, impulses, gut feelings, and tried-and-true solutions from the past. In those situations, we seldom take the time to determine what or who is influencing us and how those influences shape our interpretation of data, personal biases, and decisions. Remember, each team member will also have their own intuition that leads them to a conclusion of what is best.

Instead of this somewhat subconscious process that can be flawed, biased, and have illogical leaps, a team leader can engage the team in decision-making. Decision-making is a process of evaluating and choosing from among a set of alternatives. We need to understand the various influences on us before we can select the best type of decision strategy for the problem we are facing. Every team member needs to develop this understanding for themselves and understand how these differences influence the other team members.

MAKING DECISIONS TOGETHER THROUGH SENSEMAKING AND DECISION-MAKING METHODS

Decision-making is a process of evaluating and choosing from among a set of alternatives. Generally, this process is thought of as having two stages:

STAGE 1. EVALUATION OR SENSEMAKING: Determine the process by which you and the team will evaluate the decision to be made. How will you gather the data necessary to make an informed decision? How will you make sense of that data? What will be the process to arrive at the final set of options to decide between? In decision-making research, this process is often called *sensemaking*, and there are many models and approaches to help teams and leaders make sense prior to making a decision.

STAGE 2. DECISION OR DECISION-MAKING: Determine the process by which you and the team will make the actual decision. Will it be by popular or majority vote? Will you, as the leader, hold the ultimate responsibility? Will you engage in consensus or participatory decision-making? This is the stage most people think of and focus on with decision-making. Sometimes, a deliberate evaluation stage is very minimal or even skipped, and individuals are left on their own to make sense of the options before the decision-making moment.

Making a definitive decision as a leader with no input from team members can run the risk of making a decision influenced by one person's biases and understanding. As we learned in part 1, there's a lot we don't know that we don't know. Team members can often make excellent contributions to the evaluation stage of the decision-making process. They are a great resource when gathering information because they have relevant technical knowledge, are familiar with the project, and bring their diverse backgrounds when offering potential solutions. Group decision-making outperforms even the best individual's decision. Therefore, leveraging the team seems like a no-brainer.

But using a fully collaborative group decision-making process has its downsides. It can be time-consuming, especially if the goal (spoken or unspoken) is to identify one solution that everyone who has contributed to the process must agree to in order to move forward. It can pressure members to conform, leading to groupthink.

Groupthink describes a situation in which the group pressures the members to conform to a perceived popular viewpoint.[14] Often, a view becomes popular because it was the first idea to be shared or an influential individual is the one who initially shared the vision. As shared by Gibb Dyer and colleagues, "Usually [differences between team members and the team leader] as a cause of team ineffectiveness is obvious to the subordinates on the team and to an outside observer. Unfortunately, however, it typically is not so apparent to the team leader. Team members may feel that the best way to get along is to go along. At times, conformity may represent true acceptance of the leader's position. But at other times, it may simply represent avoidance of conflict."[15]

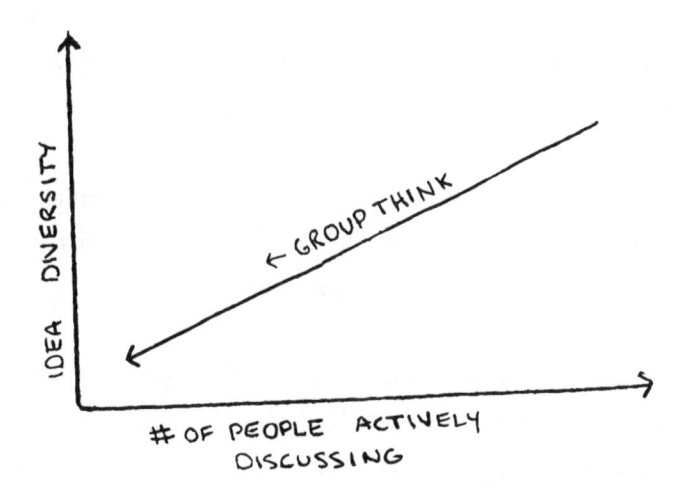

[A hand-drawn chart with the y-axis labeled "IDEA DIVERSITY" and the x-axis labeled "# OF PEOPLE ACTIVELY DISCUSSING". A diagonal line rises from lower-left to upper-right, labeled "← GROUP THINK".]

When an individual point of view differs from the dominant majority, there is a tendency to hide or doubt the individual's point of view. The greater the perceived risk for sharing alternative views, the stronger the pressure to go along to get along.

Groupthink can blind the team and inhibit the team from making a critical and thorough decision evaluation. As leaders, inviting a devil's advocate approach where alternative views are invited can break the groupthink spell to reveal whether the group's decision truly represents the team's collective wisdom and expertise.

However, decision-making processes do not have to be a choice between authoritative and 100 percent consensus. Teams can move beyond groupthink and bias by establishing team norms on how decisions are made. As shared in the "Putting the Concept into Practice" section, there are many options in between for both sensemaking and decision-making.

PUTTING THE CONCEPT INTO PRACTICE

Even though we make decisions on the fly every day at work and on teams, it's clear that there are times when decisions must be more thoughtful. It's easy to be exclusive, illogical, or biased when making decisions. The following tools can help you and your team design each stage of the process.

The first step is understanding what kind of decision-making process to use. How do you choose which process is suitable for a particular situation? Some factors you might consider are:

- How urgent is the decision that needs to be made? What is at risk for every moment of delay? If a decision is urgent, this indicates that you should choose a process that will be quicker and that will have a clear decision owner who has the authority to move forward right away.

- What is the level of risk and/or impact associated with the problem and solution? If a decision could impact many people, especially negatively, this indicates that you will want to engage in a lengthier process, with a clear evaluation stage, and gather input from many people.

The second step is designing the sensemaking method. For the evaluation stage, engage in a sensemaking process: Sensemaking generally falls along a spectrum of quantitative and qualitative data evaluation. Some common ways to work together to make sense of data are as follows:

- **BEST VALUE OPTION ANALYSIS (A "QUANTITATIVE EVALUATION" METHOD):** In this method, essential criteria for the decision are listed, such as cost, quality, time, impact, etc. Then options are generated, and details are mapped out for each measure. The team or decision owner can then compare and contrast options to make the decision more easily. Sometimes, criteria are assigned different weights, based on whether one is more important than another.

- **INVOLVEMENT AND REFLECTION SYNTHESIS PROCESS (ALSO THOUGHT OF AS "QUALITATIVE EVALUATION"):** When a decision is softer and the metric-oriented criteria are less important, perspective-gathering takes center stage. The people most affected by a decision may be consulted to get their opinions on potential solutions or to learn whether the solutions a team has come up with have faults or merits. A survey might be done to allow for some quantitative input. Then the decision owner(s) may generate and synthesize qualitative themes to arrive at solutions.

Here are some additional questions that can help you design ways to make sense of the data:

- Who has the data?

- Where and how will data be gathered to make an informed decision?

- Will you make sense of the data on your own? Who else will play a role, and how?

- What key questions will you seek to answer when you review the data? What are the relevant decision-making criteria, and why?

The third step is to pick a decision-making method. A good decision-making process strikes the best balance between time and energy spent gathering multiple perspectives and being decisive. Here are a few common decision-making processes:

- **VOTING METHODS:** There are a variety of ways to use voting to make a decision. These range from popular or majority vote to dot voting to more formal methods like Robert's Rules of Order.[16] Most people are familiar with a popular vote. Dot voting allows for a silent approach, in which members are given one or more dots and place them on the options they would like to move forward with. It's an excellent way to show where the momentum is in the room. Robert's Rules of Order focuses on making motions, allowing time for clarifying questions and debate, and then voting. Voting can be done after a thorough, deliberate evaluation process, but often it occurs more quickly, relying on an individual's knowledge and understanding.

- **CONSENSUS:** Another option is by consensus. Consensus often involves a lengthier evaluation stage where group members come up with the various options or solutions that will be then agreed upon. A lot of energy is put on making sure everyone's voices are heard and all ideas are considered. Often, concepts are blended. Consensus is often confused with needing every person to fully agree with every aspect of the final outcome.

Rather, the goal is for members to agree on an outcome that everyone can actively support or at least live with. Consensus decision-making works well when the members are cooperative and trust one another to reach a general agreement. A Consent-Based Decision-Making Process is one example of a consensus-style process and follows the steps below.

- Proposal: The item owner makes the decision.

- Question (to all): Do you have any questions to clarify what you just heard?

- Reaction: What's working about this proposal? How would you improve the proposal?

- Clarify and amend: The item owner can clarify and/or amend the proposal.

- Objection: Do you have data that indicates this is unsafe to try for our business?

- Integration (optional): What can be added or changed to remove that objection?

- **OWNER-BASED DECISION-MAKING:** In this option, prior to gathering or evaluating any data, it's made clear who owns the decision. In this process, some individuals are usually tasked with generating options or providing input. These perspectives are then assembled into proposals that are presented to the decision owner. The decision owner then makes the call. This works well when the decision to be made involves a high risk, little time, and an apparent authority (e.g., a person who will be signing the check or contract once the decision is made). You might refer back to your team charter for the agreements around roles. If not in your team charter, you can use other tools. The EDITS framework is one example of a method for choosing who should be responsible for making the decision.

- Expertise and experiences: Who has the knowledge and experiences related to this decision?

- Data: Who has the most reliable access to data and information about this decision?

- Impact: Who is most affected by this decision?

- Time: Who has the time and energy to make this decision?

- Skill: Who has the skill to solicit and integrate advice when needed?

A STEM METAPHOR TO DRIVE THE POINT HOME: IF/THEN STATEMENTS

In programming, logic is always used to choose the next step. Input is obtained, assessed, and then a decision is made for the output. For example, if/then statements in programming say if x is received, then y is the result.

Although human decision-making processes are more complex (and less rational), we follow a similar process of taking in data, assessing it, and then deciding on an output action. The difference is that we each have our own programming. Group sensemaking and decision-making are analogous to a meta program that integrates the outputs and logic of individual programming into one outcome. Each group has the choice of what integrating logic to use—and this is often the work of leaders. Leaders guide the creation of the group logic and work to integrate individual approaches and move the team towards action.

A STORY IN ACTION

Katia and her technician team oversee nuclear reactor plants. During a maintenance shutdown, an instrument technician reported a discrepancy with the seals on the nuclear fuel shutoff valves. The seals had been replaced just six months ago, so it was surprising that they needed to be replaced again. The team realized no seals were available in the warehouse and that ordering new ones would exceed the typically allowable shutdown timeline.

Katia asked the team for their input while acknowledging the enormous pressure on all of them to avoid exceeding the shutdown timeline. She asked the team what they would do in her position. Some of the team members questioned the instrument technician's conclusion because the seals were only six months old and the manufacturer's recommendation was to replace them every eighteen months. Some felt it was a no-brainer to replace the faulty shutoff valves because of the potential risk of releasing toxins into the environment, which would impact the community.

Referring back to the team charter, she reviewed the participatory decision-making rules they had agreed to. They had all agreed that the team owned the decisions, so the entire team was engaged in evaluating the situation. They decided to research all possible alternatives, both conventional and outside-the-box options. The team thought it would be important to consult with the manufacturer of the seals, the production planning team, and other plants. They worked through several alternatives and realized that the manufacturer could not ship new seals before the shutdown timeline ended. They learned from the production planning team that there weren't any other scheduled downtimes coming up that they could leverage. They also learned that another plant had a spare set of seals that could be shipped and used, but sending the seals would cause that plant to be at risk. After a great deal of discussion that generated many creative ideas, they decided they needed to send the issue to people higher up in the organization since it involved multiple sites outside of the team's influence.

Katia was hesitant but agreed because it was the team's decision. She reported this discrepancy to her boss, and the decision-making process rose to a new level. Using the insights the team had already gathered, her boss used her relationships to work with the plant manager at the other location to obtain their seals and get new seals rushed from the manufacturer. Her boss also tasked the production planning team with finding the optimal time for a shutdown to install the new seals. Lastly, Katia and her team were tasked with leading a root cause analysis to understand what went wrong to prevent this issue in the future. Since Katia and the team worked on this problem together, they all contributed a tremendous number of insights about this mishap and were able to identify other potential related risks.

REFLECTION QUESTIONS

- Who or what is most influential in your life?
- How does this influence impact your decision-making?
- What strategies have you used in the past? What made them successful?

- Do you tend to make decisions on the fly or shooting from the hip—in other words, immediately from your intuition? How about your team(s)? What are the pros and cons of this approach?

- When might it make sense to forego a detailed decision-making process?

- Can you think of a time when you engaged in a deliberate sensemaking or evaluation process? What was it like?

- What do you want the decision-making process to look like for your team(s)? How and when might you share your thoughts with your team?

FURTHER READING AND REFERENCES

On the more casual side . . . books and resources to check out:

American Psychological Association. (2022). "Groupthink." https://dictionary.apa.org/groupthink.

Dyer, W. Gibb, Jr., Jeffrey H. Dyer, and William G. Dyer. (2013). *Team Building: Proven Strategies for Improving Team Performance.*

On the more academic side . . . references we used:

Clifton, Jim, and Jim Harter. (2019). *It's the Manager: Moving from Boss to Coach.*

Peters, Tom. (1987). *Thriving on Chaos: Handbook for a Management Revolution.*

Robert III, H. M., T. J. Honemann, T .J. Balch, D. E. Seabold, and S. Gerber. (2020) *Robert's Rules of Order.*

4.5

CELEBRATING TEAMWORK | CLOSINGS, FEEDFORWARD, AND RETROSPECTIVES

The more you celebrate your life, the more there is in life to celebrate.

—OPRAH WINFREY

THE PROBLEM	• Do you or your team consistently just move on to the next thing instead of pausing to celebrate accomplishments?
These are just *some* of the challenges you might encounter that including celebrations helps solve.	• Do you sense feelings of burnout or underappreciation in yourself or your team members?

How often does the work of STEM professionals go unnoticed because we don't want to jinx it? Or because we want to move ahead and start solving the subsequent problem? So much of the great work you are doing is underrated, undervalued, or invisible in organizations because of this very reason. Next thing you know, you are being asked to do the next project faster, with less material, and with more high-profile solutions. Most nontechnical professionals have little experience understanding the deep work that goes into the many solutions produced by the technical community—many of which create benefits for society at large.

For example, one of the most outstanding engineers of all time was Nikola Tesla.[17] He was originally from Serbia, and when he was in his late twenties, he moved to the United States to work with Thomas Edison. Tesla's work was underappreciated during his lifetime, and he never received credit for several of his contributions. His considerable contributions to society include the induction motor, three-phase electricity, fluorescent lighting, and the Tesla coil. He also developed an alternating current (electric current that flows in the reverse direction) generation system made from a transformer and a motor. (Alternating current competed with direct current technology, which was more popular at the time.) It wasn't until 2003, long after Tesla passed away, that Elon Musk and others brought recognition to his name by calling their new company Tesla Motors—an appropriate name for the company that may become the most successful car manufacturer of the future.[18]

Contributions and team success should never have to be overshadowed by fear of what happens if it doesn't work. For you and your team to feel motivated and recognized, celebrations are key activities to engage in. All technical work, even if it still isn't perfect and has setbacks, is an essential contribution to industry and society's evolution. Celebrations, closings, and reflection are critical tools that provide a sense of satisfaction and help build momentum for the next adventure for your team.

CELEBRATING TEAMWORK

Celebration is a kind of food we all need in our lives, and each individual brings a special recipe or offering so that together we will make a great feast. It is richer and fuller when many work and then celebrate together.

—KENT AND STEWARD, *LEARNING BY HEART*

Recognizing and celebrating individual and team success is a powerful motivator because it reinforces the countless hours and hard work necessary to make progress and achieve the team's goals. In addition, celebrating accomplishments is a way of appreciating the ways in which the team's achievements contribute to scientific knowledge and, potentially, to solving larger problems faced by humanity. Showing appreciation to each team member and recognizing their contribution not only is an important part of team cohesion but also elevates the individual's sense of self-worth and increases their confidence in their abilities.

Celebrations, closings, and retrospectives don't have to be restricted only to the formal end of a project. Celebrating key project milestones can provide essential motivation to keep moving forward, especially if the team is facing challenges on the next stage of a project.

Celebration is a simple idea and should be fun! And here are some guidelines to make them even easier:

Track success and celebrate small(ish) wins. As a leader, it is important to be vigilant and know how individual team members are doing and how well the team is working together. Knowing the key project milestones, which would have been established in the team charter, can help a leader gauge where the team is in the process and provide an opportunity to encourage team members about the progress made to date. This is not to say that you need to have a party for every inch the project moves forward. It's about identifying ways to stay motivated. Research tells us that individual team members and teams as a whole will expend the most energy at the beginning and the end of a project.[19]

The problem lies in motivating the one thousand steps in between the beginning and the end. Rallying the team during lulls, especially at milestones, helps the team to see that constant and consistent good work pays off.

Know when the team is in a lull. The leader needs to be sensitive to the team's energy and know when the team is in a lull. There are some easy indicators.

IS YOUR TEAM IN A LULL?

CONTINUE TO INVESTIGATE ←NO— { is your team in alignment? / is your team learning something new? / is your team well rested? (not fatigued) } —YES→ STEP BACK & CELEBRATE

1. The first is when the team starts to turn on itself. This might look like a typical difference of opinions, but can signal deeper divisions or a lack of alignment. At such moments, a leader

who is tuned in to their team can help the team members reset and celebrate where the team has come from and where they are heading.

2. The second is when people who are usually excited about the work start to show signs of fatigue. In such moments, a reset or work timeout is needed to regain a sense of purpose in the midst of all the detailed work.

3. The third is when people become bored or unenthusiastic about their work. In such cases, they may need the excitement of learning something new that will add to the success of the process. Although it might seem like adding more to their plate or taking them away from the task at hand, learning is a great way to engage people's brains and get them excited to apply their new knowledge to the project.

Celebrating the end. Most often, teams simply disband, and the individuals move on to the next problem at the end of a project. Instead of letting the team disintegrate, consider different ways to recognize and reflect on the work achieved:

- Highlight the team's work with upper leadership or use public avenues like department meetings to recognize the team's work.

- Have a team celebration—an outing or a virtual reflection focused on having fun.

- Engage in a debrief—take time to reflect on what everyone learned and say goodbye to each other (if everyone will be moving to different projects) or to the project.

In the "Putting the Concept into Practice" section, you'll find a few specific tools to use during milestones, during lulls, and at the end of projects.

PUTTING THE CONCEPT INTO PRACTICE

Perspective will come in retrospect.   —MELODY BEATTIE

Hindsight is always 20/20. Therefore, at the end of a project, reflecting on all that you experience during the project is a good way to be reminded that nothing worth doing is without challenges. Here are a couple of approaches to help structure celebrations and debrief events:

- **GIVE TIME FOR FEEDFORWARD**: Feedforward, coined and championed by Marshall Goldsmith, is an alternative to feedback. It helps us notice what we could do in the future based on what we have learned in the present. As Goldsmith shares, "How people are doing is information commonly given in 360-degree feedback, but such feedback focuses on past events—not on the infinite possibilities of the future. Feedforward assumes that people can make positive changes in the future, whereas feedback tends to reinforce stereotyping, self-fulfilling prophecies, and feelings of failure."[20] This is how it sounds different. Feedback asks the question "What could I have done better?" which inherently asks for comparison to past performance. To feedforward, simply answer the question "What can be of help in the future?"

- **GRATITUDE GIVING**: In the end, gratefulness is the only appropriate response to the amazing challenges faced by the team and the perseverance exhibited by the team members that drove the project to completion. In breakout rooms, one-on-one, or through online channels, your team can express gratitude to one another.

- **RETROSPECTIVES:** Popular in the Agile community, retrospectives are all about learning from what happened and then focusing on what to do differently in the future. There are many sites that provide different formats for creating engaging retrospectives, such as FunRetrospectives.com. As Agile coach Michael de le Maza says, "Sometimes it feels like your team is on a hamster wheel. But, what if you were to step off that wheel periodically? Maybe you'd realize that a little grease makes things a whole lot easier. Those periodic opportunities to evaluate your work are the magic behind retrospectives."[21]

A STORY IN ACTION

Last night was the go-live for a team's latest software feature. Within minutes, a surge of emails came in about the bugs in the programming. The team had anticipated the what-ifs that could go wrong and had quick solutions ready. However, the team realized that, with the high number of initial issues reported, there was a high probability of more problems, so they remained constantly on the lookout.

The team was exhausted. They had been working on the project nonstop leading up to the go-live date and had had no time to pause at all, much less pause and appreciate the work they had done. Although they were glad the software was launched, the team members had reached the limits of their capacity as they prepared for the true stress testing by live customers.

Alex, the team lead, was busy managing the team's reaction to the software release. He reminded them that no software is without bugs and that what makes a launch successful is how the team responds to the bugs. To redirect the team's focus from what was going wrong, he highlighted all the successful team milestones they had celebrated that had led up to this point.

He also reminded them of how the team had joked about the launch bugs and how they were going to "crush them bugs." Once the team was reminded of all that they had accomplished and that, even with the bugs, they had a backup plan, they realized how great the software was. They took a moment on their next call to appreciate each other and everyone's contributions and expressed specific moments they were grateful for.

REFLECTION QUESTIONS

- How frequently do you celebrate your personal successes?
- What are ways you and the team members keep each other motivated?
- When the team is struggling, what do you do to celebrate wins or show each other appreciation?
- In what ways do you actively get closure when work is done?

FURTHER READING AND REFERENCES

On the more casual side . . . books and resources to check out:

> InnerDrive. (2022). "Why the Middle Is the Hardest Part of a Task." https://blog.innerdrive.co.uk/middle-hardest-part-of-task.

Beattie, Melody. (2022). "Today's Daily Meditation." https://melodybeattie.com/perspective.

Goldsmith, Marshall. (Undated). "FeedForward." http://www.marshallgoldsmithfeedforward.com/html/FeedForward-Tool.htm.

Gregersen, Erik. (2021). "Tesla, Inc." Britannica. https://www.britannica.com/topic/Tesla-Motors.

Editors, History.com. (2020). "Nikola Tesla." https://www.history.com/topics/inventions/nikola-tesla.

Kent, Corita, and Jan Steward. (2008). *Learning By Heart: Teaching to Free the Creative Spirit*.

de la Maza, Michael. (2020). "The Guide to Retrospectives—Remote or in Person." Miro. https://miro.com/guides/retrospectives.

PART 5

$$N = \frac{X_1}{\sum_{i-n}^{n} x_i + \sum_{i-n}^{n} y_i}$$

THE FIRST PRINCIPLES OF LEADING TEAMS OF TEAMS

In part 4, we focused on team leadership—project teams or work teams where leadership roles are informally taken on or formally assigned. In this part, we progress to formally managing others as well as leading teams of teams.

The progression from leading yourself to leading teams to now leading teams of teams is a seismic shift in priorities. The self-focused priorities in the earlier stages of your career are still present but are no longer front and center—the measures of success change from enabling personal success towards enabling the success of other people and the organization. When the success measures change, so do the key tasks and responsibilities that you focus on. Rather than focusing on what you can directly control when leading yourself, now you focus on how you can influence and direct others.

With little to no notice or discussion, as a leader or manager, you might have noticed that there's an expectation you will have a rich psychological understanding of people; you are also expected to know how to apply that understanding to help others in the organization. For example, many articles have been written about how successful leaders have high emotional intelligence, empathy, and compassion. With every published article comes a high expectation that leaders have this innate sense of when people are experiencing emotional distress and that leaders inherently know the right moves to alleviate that distress. These expectations are unrealistic. In most organizations, managers are first and foremost promoted or hired to run day-to-day business operations and think strategically about the organization's future. While most leaders are excited about empowering and developing employees, they often, through no fault of their own, lack the organizational support to develop these people skills. Furthermore, when leaders do receive support, it is often one-size-fits-all, despite the fact that each leader probably has different skills they need to improve.

> ### CONNECT BACK TO WHY
>
> One of the greatest challenges facing the global community is environmental sustainability and climate change. The global scale of this challenge is beginning to spark global collaboration. As stated in the research article "Sustainability and Collaboration," "Increased involvement in teamwork is driven in no small part by the scale and complexity of scientific and societal problems, including challenges to sustainability as well as health and peace."[1] Navigating such transorganizational relationships to effect change is a new horizon for STEM professionals.

In this part, we empower leaders to develop their capability to align their people to the business strategy. We cover the following topics:

- **MAKING SENSE OF THE ORGANIZATION (PAGE 231):** We introduce the theories of open systems and complex systems to help you understand the bigger picture and context you are operating within.

- **WORKING WITH THE CULTURE (PAGE 244):** You will learn about the Beach and STAR models to help you articulate the culture and develop a strategy.

- **MOTIVATING AND ENGAGING PEOPLE (PAGE 254):** You will learn how to use both intrinsic and extrinsic factors to encourage your team to perform at a high level.

- **NAVIGATING INTERNAL POLITICS (PAGE 263):** You will learn how to build cross-organizational relationships and navigate organizational defensive routines.

- **CULTIVATING COLLECTIVE WISDOM (PAGE 275):** How to learn from the organization.

In other words, in this part, we will explore ways to zoom out to understand and work with the organization as a dynamic ecosystem.

FURTHER READING AND REFERENCES

On the more academic side . . . a reference we used:

Klein, J. T. "Sustainability and Collaboration: Cross-Disciplinary and Cross-Sector Horizons." *Sustainability*. https://doi.org/10.3390/su12041515.

5.1

MAKING SENSE OF THE ORGANIZATION | OPEN AND COMPLEX SYSTEM THEORIES

Leadership is a difficult practice personally because it almost always requires you to make a challenging adaptation yourself. What makes adaptation complicated is that it involves deciding what is so essential that it must be preserved going forward and what of all that you value can be left behind. Those are hard choices because they involve both protecting what is most important to you and bidding adieu to something you previously held dear: a relationship, a value, an idea, an image of yourself.

—RONALD A. HEIFETZ AND COLLEAGUES,
The Practice of Adaptive Leadership

THE PROBLEM These are just *some* of the challenges you might encounter that stepping back and analyzing the whole system helps solve.	• Do you feel like you don't get the organization or haven't had the time to figure it out? • Do you often feel like you get stuck in the weeds and are overwhelmed by managing the day-to-day details? • Do you struggle to work on the most meaningful tasks? Do you wonder whether you are spending your time well? • Do you feel like you can't give clear and impactful direction to your team(s)?

Whether you're managing a single team, a department of teams, or multiple departments, aligning the collective knowledge, tasks, and skills of your people with the business goals is an ongoing challenge for all organizations. As a leader, a core part of your role now includes establishing the vision and setting the strategy for your team, department, or organization. But this can be easier said than done.

In your new role, you might be feeling the gnawing anxiety that comes from dealing with a large number of moving parts and the amplified complexity of leadership. The fundamental people skills we have explored thus far remain relevant to your own job performance. But now in your leadership position, you oversee many people who are navigating their own challenges of self-leadership as they work with others. Just like within yourself and with individual team members, teams of teams and even large departments have competing ideas and priorities that can cause inertia when trying to produce desired outcomes. At each level, from individuals up to large departments, entities can jump reactively to conclusions, have blind spots, express conflicts, have power struggles, bring unique strengths, and more.

Sometimes, you might find yourself as a team lead or department head who is in the weeds and has to manage the day-to-day work process. This poses another challenge to setting strategy. Being on the dance floor, as discussed in part 4.1, you could miss the crucial context of the business and, therefore, the consequences of decisions you make.

As a new leader, you may be eager to come in and make your own mark based on past experiences or a desire to stand out and revolutionize the way things have been done. But be aware of falling into a myopic point of view. Your reliance on what you know from past experiences may prevent you from seeing the entirety of the new, bigger picture that you are now responsible for.

In all these scenarios, a core skill to develop is to step back from the details on the dance floor and get a bigger view from the balcony. By getting on the balcony, you avoid getting stuck in the organized chaos of the dance floor. You can take a more expansive view of what is going on, what is important, what the available resources are, and how to use them together so that the rising tide lifts all boats. In other words, you can focus on improvements that will benefit the entire organization.

MAKING SENSE OF THE ORGANIZATION THROUGH OPEN AND COMPLEX SYSTEM THEORIES

Let's talk about ways you can make sense of your organization so you can form an effective strategy. We'll start by describing Porter's frameworks, which are two standard strategy development models used by marketing and business leaders to make sense of their organizations.

Porter's Four Strategies and Five Forces are two frameworks that focus on analyzing a business against its external environment to determine its competitive advantage.[2] Even though you might not be the CEO, it is crucial for you to know your organization's overall competitive advantage because it will help you understand the priorities that govern the decisions made above your level.

According to Michael Porter, there are four general strategies to achieve a competitive advantage.[3] These strategies have two dimensions: market scope and competitive scope. Your organization's market scope could be broad or narrow. The competitive scope could be based on low costs or high differentiation (think uniqueness). This creates four possible strategies that can be expressed in a two-by-two matrix. Where do you think your organization, department, or product line fits? Where your organization falls in this matrix will influence the structures needed to effectively mobilize the teams of teams to reach the company's larger goals.

	COSTS	DIFFERENTIATION
INDUSTRY	MOST COMPETITIVE IN COST OVERALL	DISTINCTIVE & UNIQUE AS A WHOLE
SEGMENT	COST FOCUSED IN A PARTICULAR PRODUCT OR NICHE	DIFFERENTIATED WITH A PARTICULAR PRODUCT OR NICHE

market scope (rows)

competitive advantage (columns)

If you are in a new start-up or if your business is trying to pivot, Porter's Five Forces may be a useful tool for analyzing and selecting a new strategy. In the Five Forces concept, a leader or leadership team assesses the threat of new entrants, the bargaining power of suppliers, the threat of substitute products, and the bargaining power of buyers. The team then determines which of the four strategies to pursue.

Porter's models help business leaders look at their competitive advantage against external organizations, but internal organizational forces are left out of the equation. This is where your role as an internal functional leader comes into play—how do you lead your people so their everyday actions are in alignment with the business strategy? As Gareth Morgan in *Images of Organization* explains, "Our theories of organizational life are built on metaphors that lead us to see and understand organizations in distinct and partial ways. Many of our taken-for-granted ideas about organizations are metaphorical. For example, we frequently talk about organizations as if they were machines . . . as a result of this kind of thinking, we often attempt to organize and manage them in a mechanistic way, forcing their human qualities into a background role."[4]

Two additional theories help us move beyond Porter's models to make sense of the organization: Open Systems Theory (a general framework developed to diagnose organizations and their fit with their goals) and Complexity Theory (a newer relationship- and pattern-oriented model).

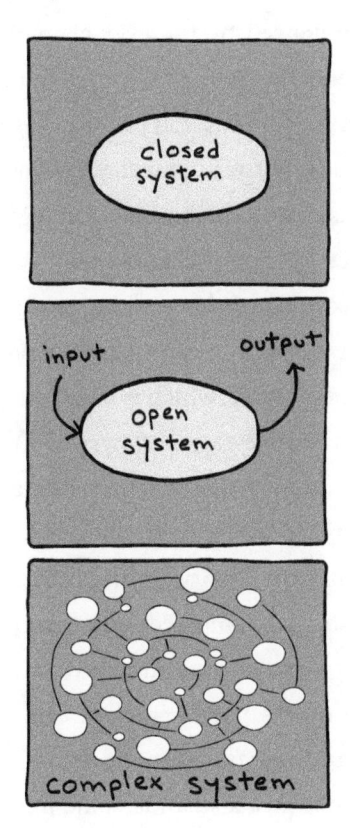

In Open Systems Theory, we acknowledge that a highly functional organization is an active ecosystem of individuals, teams, and departments interacting in a physical and virtual environment.[5] The organizational ecosystem has inputs, outputs, and transformations that happen in between the input and output. The system relies on feedback loops as the outcomes of past actions influence the data input for future actions. When you look at an organization from an *open* standpoint, you are acknowledging that your team or department is not self-contained—it has external influences. (A system without external influences would be a *closed* system.)

An open system is highly permeable and allows interaction between its internal and external influences. Since all organizations are open systems, they are influenced by the ever-changing business environment (external influence) and the needs of each individual (the internal ecosystem). As a leader, one way you can use this theory is to map the inputs, transformations, outputs, and the feedback you're getting and compare this information to the business strategy. In the "Putting the Concept into Practice" section, we'll see how to complete an open systems assessment of your team, department, or organization.

One of the latest views of leadership and strategy formation is the Complexity Theory of Change, which is based on quantum physics and chaos theory, rather than Newtonian physics.[6] While Systems Theory is helpful, it has limitations (just like Newtonian physics) in that it focuses on parts that add up linearly to a whole and tends towards a static strategy. Complexity Theory, on the other hand, focuses on the in-between relationships. It embraces emergence and dynamism as a natural part of strategy and change and moves away from simple cause and effect assumptions. As put by ancient Sufi teaching, "You think because you understand *one* you must understand *two*, because one and one make two. But you must also understand *and*."

Stepping back and looking at your organization or team from a complexity point of view allows you to embrace the possibility of continuous innovation. A complexity point of view can help you see how small changes create large effects as part of your strategy and direction setting. And this approach can relieve some of the burden of leadership. Rather than focusing on control as the tool to drive production, we embrace direction and emergence to achieve productivity and effectiveness. This contrasts with old concepts of leadership, as Margaret Wheatley describes in her book *Leadership and the New Science*: "Newton's world of cause and effect, of force acting upon force, required great expenditures of personal energy to get someone else moving, vast regions of space to traverse to get something done."[7]

Here are a few of the principles of the Complexity Theory of Change:

- Focus on creating an understanding of the whole and the relationships between parts, rather than processing the parts.

- Small interactions can create quantum leaps—change is about critical connections rather than critical mass.

- Predictability is a myth. Probability and potentials are reality.

- We can help create and set strange attractors—simple invisible rules of the system that initially seem to create chaos but in reality guide patterns over time.

- Less control leads to more order, promotes self-organization based on a clear sense of identity, *and* creates the freedom to act on it.

- Reality is co-created when we observe it and is based on *who* observes it—objectivity is a myth.

By focusing your strategy on harnessing the relationships and spaces between people and the potential each person has to deliver on their part of the business strategy, your tactics shift from micromanaging the parts to establishing the deeper values and goals for the people you are leading. In "Putting the Concept into Practice," we take a look at how to step back and view your organization through a complexity lens.

There are many ways to assess an organization and then create a plan to move it towards a new set of future goals. These are just three approaches you might use to review your organization when you step onto the balcony and create your vision for your team, department, or larger unit.

PUTTING THE CONCEPT INTO PRACTICE

If you choose to try an open system approach to understanding your organization, the process is relatively simple. First, decide on the right level for your analysis. Are you leading a team? A department or function made up of multiple teams? Multiple departments? This is your unit of analysis. Then, jot down the answers to the following questions for your unit of analysis:

- **INPUTS:** What are the main resources coming into your unit? What information, raw materials, energy, and people are given to your unit to work with?

- **TRANSFORMATION:** What are the main technologies used to transform the inputs to outputs? What roles and organizational structures are vital? What management processes and HR systems guide and incentivize transformation? What is the current strategy and culture?

- **OUTPUTS:** What are the results your unit is measured on? How do you know your unit is effective? What financial, productivity, or satisfaction (external customer, internal stakeholder, or employee) metrics are important?

After listing these out, look at the feedback you have on how well your unit is performing. If you don't already have feedback, collect it! Information sharing increases everyone's ability to become more aware of trends that might become problems in the near future. The more information (feedback) leaders get from more people, the better the inputs are for future decision-making.

Based on your analysis of the feedback received, and perhaps working with key leaders or influencers in or above your unit, what do you think needs to change to increase performance? This is where your strategy begins. You will then move from strategy to specific tactics to create forward progress.

If you opt for the complexity view in addition to or instead of the open systems approach, here are a few steps you can take to form a strategy.

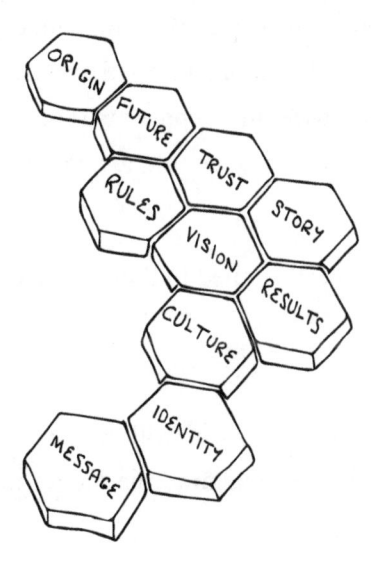

1. What is the origin story for your unit? What past leaders or past events have influenced the current culture? What rules or patterns in behavior do you observe as a result of those influences?

2. What are the results your unit is achieving, and what is your organization calling for in the future?

3. What other in-between-the-lines or hidden-below-the-surface messages are your unit receiving?

4. What are the few simple rules and values that need to be embodied to achieve the next wave of progress? Remember, the Complexity Theory of Change says that your job is not to make sure people know exactly what to do and when to do it. Instead, by establishing the vision, shaping the core identity, and trusting your people, you will give them the autonomy they need to achieve their goals.

5. This is key: Who will you work with as you identify your vision for your team, department, or team of teams? In order to create an intelligent organization, we need to collaborate on the plan. Otherwise, all it represents is one person's experience and interpretation of something too complex and dynamic to be accurate.

6. What do you need to shed in order to adapt to your new vision?

By following these steps, you will create a new strategy. And your next step will be to determine the tactics needed to carry out the strategy.

A STEM METAPHOR TO DRIVE THE POINT HOME: FROM NEWTONIAN TO QUANTUM PHYSICS

Moving from an open systems lens to a Complexity Theory lens is the same progression science makes when moving from Newtonian to quantum physics. In a Newtonian world, we tried to understand nature by breaking everything into ever smaller parts. And the smaller parts were microcosms of the bigger parts. The world was a predictable place of cause and effect. In a quantum world, we realized the spaces in between the parts are crucial, and that in those spaces only probabilities and potentials can be assessed, rather than predictable answers. Early organizational theory began to understand the organization as a simple machine. Now we have progressed to understanding organizations as living, dynamic, complex systems.

A STORY IN ACTION

Jonas recently was promoted and is now the supervisor of a department that comprises several teams. Excited to impress his boss and peers, he would often promote his department and shared their successes widely. But he also frequently compared his department to other departments.

At first, his peers were excited about his success. But eventually they started to notice that he had little understanding of the larger context of the information he was sharing. Jonas seemed to be operating his department as if it was its own organization instead of part of the larger whole.

At the next quarterly meeting, his peer Patricia shared that her department was in a downturn with production. As she described possible reasons for the downturn, Jonas realized that some of the actions of people in his department were undermining her department. After the meeting, Jonas started mapping out the inputs and outputs of his team and started thinking about the interdependencies that would make his team *and* the entire organization successful.

Later, he approached Patricia to discuss possible ways to collaborate. Jonas realized he lacked the business acumen he needed to effectively lead his department and that he had been simply continuing to work in the same patterns he had followed before. But after using Complexity Theory to assess his department's performance, both his and Patricia's departments were soon outperforming their prior quarter results. As a consequence of their successful efforts, Jonas and Patricia encouraged the other department heads to take a complex systems approach to analyzing collaboration among departments.

REFLECTION QUESTIONS

- What else would you like to learn about how your team fits into the organization as a whole?

- Apply the concept of the Johari Window on a larger scale—what don't you know about the organization? What do you guess you don't know that you don't know?

- What assumptions have you made so far, based on your past experience, about what's important to your organization, what outside factors are influencing its strategy, and how things get done?

- How might these assumptions need to change or shift based on what you see from your new level?

FURTHER READING AND REFERENCES

On the more casual side . . . books and resources to check out:

Harvard Business Review interview with Michael E. Porter. (2008). "The Five Competitive Forces that Shape Strategy." https://www.youtube.com/watch?v=mYF2_FBCvXw.

Heifetz, Ronald A., Marty Linsky, and Alexander Grashow. (2009). *The Practice of Adaptive Leadership: Tools and Tactics for Changing Your Organization and the World.*

On the more academic side . . . references we used:

Cummings, Thomas G., and Christopher G. Worley. (2018). *Organization Development and Change.*

Morgan, Gareth. (2006). *Images of Organization.*

Porter, Michael E. (1985). *Competitive Advantage.*

Wheatley, Margaret J. (2006). *Leadership and the New Science: Discovering Order in a Chaotic World.*

5.2

WORKING WITH THE CULTURE | THE BEACH AND STAR MODELS

Culture and leadership are two sides of the same coin, and one cannot understand one without the other.

—EDGAR SCHEIN, *The Corporate Culture Survival Guide*

THE PROBLEM	• Do you feel like there's something invisible getting in the way of change and achievement?
These are just *some* of the challenges you might encounter that working with the culture helps solve.	• Do you want to make a change to the culture but don't know how?
	• Do you want to find ways to work with the culture and use it better to achieve the goals of the organization?

As managers and leaders, you wear many hats. You are responsible for not only increasing productivity by motivating your employees and reducing expenses but also reinforcing the organization's culture. Organizational culture emerges from a set of core values, beliefs, and assumptions initially established by the founder(s) of the organization. Although the culture is established by the founder(s), over time, it gains momentum and takes on a life of its own. The founder's values, beliefs, and assumptions expand and shift as the organization grows, employees come and go, successes and failures occur, and the market landscape becomes more competitive. The longer an organization has been around, the more its culture is characterized by deeply entrenched norms of "how things are done around here."

It's not enough to follow or even help shape the business strategy. Aligning your team or teams with the business strategy and creating the right culture for the work to get done is an inevitable part of your job. This is the case regardless of whether you personally agree or disagree with aspects of the company culture. You might even spend most of your day having conversations that start with "that's how we have always done it."

Culture is created and recreated at every level of the organization. It is reinforced and created by each individual. But because managers interact with employees on a day-to-day basis and hold positional power, they have a lot of influence on their employees at the individual (psychological) level. In fact, 70 percent of the variance in team engagement is determined solely by the manager.[8] The number one reason people give for leaving their company is because of their manager. These exits happen for several reasons, but the primary reason is that a manager has created a negative culture—this is the downside to the fact that managers have significant control over the climate they create for their employees. As you interact with your team or department, the climate will emerge within the pre-existing, and perhaps emerging, culture. During this process, it's critical to avoid building a toxic climate where behaviors contradict a healthy climate or desired organizational culture. Toxic behaviors are often demonstrated as a "my way or the highway" attitude. On the flip side, it's common for a particular team or department to have its own positive culture that stands out from the rest of the organization. You can have a significant influence on your team or department and create beneficial anomalies from the norm if you choose.

In this topic, we discuss how you can foster a positive collective climate (a shared perspective with other teams and departments) and support a healthy organizational culture as a whole.

WORKING WITH THE CULTURE BY USING THE BEACH MODEL

As Edgar Schein explains in the first edition of his book *The Corporate Culture Survival Guide*, leaders typically choose among four options when they join an organization: destroy the existing culture, fight the existing culture, give in to the existing culture, or evolve the culture. Here, we are focused on the fourth option, which is often the most productive one.

DESTROY   FIGHT   GIVE IN   EVOLVE

To build a climate that synchronizes well with the overall organizational culture, you first need to understand your organization's culture in general. For this task, in the third edition of the guide, Edgar and Peter Schein share the metaphor of a beach as a model for culture. At first, you might visualize a relaxing vacation! But, of course, culture is much more complex and dynamic. Shift your imagination to where the waves break against the shore. That's where our metaphor begins.

In their model, an organization's culture is represented by the beach itself. Just like a beach, an organization has an originating set of factors and environmental conditions that determine its initial shape. But, just like a beach, the story doesn't end there. The culture isn't static.

Consider that a beach is always in the process of being made. It was, is, and is becoming, just like a community's culture. As Edgar and Peter Schein say, "A myth we should abandon is that culture is 'something' that can be easily built, managed, and manipulated by leaders and 'champions' to create 'positive change' over the course of a sprint, hackathon, quarterly initiative, or even annual planning cycle."[9] Culture is dynamic and changes grain by grain.

What changes the beach? What forces are at work? At scale, the winds blowing from the ocean to the beach might represent external forces coming to change the beach. At an individual scale, imagine a leader and their leadership actions or initiatives as an individual wave or collection of waves. You, as a leader, may have a vision or idea and come with momentum to your task. Over time, as you traverse your network in the organization with your vision and actions, you build momentum until you break your change on the shore of the broader community. The beach changes, even if in only a small way. The impact you've made feeds back to you and creates a pull back to the ocean—the *backwash*—refueling you for your next wave of iteration.

When you observe a wave, you probably notice how little changes with each wave breaking. There's a lot of resistance present as well. The same is true with culture. The tailwind isn't the only wind blowing. Imagine the *headwind*, the wind blowing from the shore to the ocean. These winds represent the resistance to change. Organizational resistance can take many forms, many of which we've covered previously.

When viewed from this lens, it becomes obvious why the most generative option for leaders is to work on evolving the culture. It's quite a feat to move sand; to destroy or fight the existing culture is an uneconomic use of effort at best and futile at worst. Though not impossible (we've all heard or experienced firsthand the actions of a toxic leader who drives a tractor through the tranquil beach of our organization), it comes at great cost. The Beach Model allows us to understand the complexity and thoughtful action required to positively change culture.

PUTTING THE CONCEPT INTO PRACTICE

The STAR Model is a great way to shape the waves or initiatives you would like to lead to impact the culture.[10]

GALBRAITH'S STAR MODEL

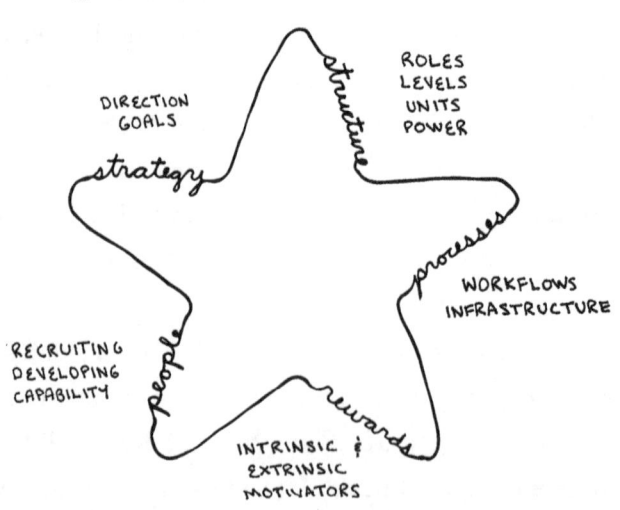

strategy — DIRECTION, GOALS

structure — ROLES, LEVELS, UNITS, POWER

processes — WORKFLOWS, INFRASTRUCTURE

rewards — INTRINSIC & EXTRINSIC MOTIVATORS

people — RECRUITING, DEVELOPING, CAPABILITY

Galbraith's STAR Model breaks down the elements that create and reinforce culture and represents those elements as the five points of a star. Often, culture change fails because a change is made only in one of the five points. All five points must be considered and aligned to truly change a culture. Just as the contours of a beach can only change when all factors—the tailwinds, the headwinds, the grains of the beach, the currents, the waves—change, your initiatives will only be successful if you consider organizational elements together (and with others involved, of course!).

1. **STRATEGY** is the organization's direction and how it will drive the results necessary to achieve the strategy. This point of the model is paramount as all of the other components cascade from the organization's strategy for being in business.

2. **STRUCTURE** is the organization's design—the defined roles, levels, and units used to deliver the work effectively.

3. **PROCESSES** are the workflows and infrastructure that are in place to create the products or services of the units.

4. **REWARDS** focus on ways the organization can acknowledge and motivate its employees, both intrinsically (such as appreciation) and extrinsically (such as wages and salary).

5. **PEOPLE** includes both hiring the right talent and developing the right skills in the people you have. These skills go much deeper than just having the right technical abilities. Having people who are aligned with the organization's values is also key to career longevity and satisfaction.

To assess each element of the STAR Model, consider applying the beach metaphor.

What are the tailwinds and headwinds bringing for each element? In other words, what external forces are driving change and what are the greatest resisting forces? Don't forget the role of the origin story in the dynamics. Look at the founder's fundamental values, beliefs, and assumptions about the direction of the business, what would drive success, and what values they expected employees to hold. Knowing which parts of the founder's fundamentals are still in place and which ones have shifted will help you discover the origins of "that's the way we have always done it" attitudes. Understand the business history: What was the problem it was solving, the business landscape it was entering, and the customers it was marketing to? What successes and failures did the business have? How did leaders react and respond? All of these factors helped create the values, beliefs, and assumptions that were operationalized over time. Some of these may contribute to the headwinds, while others might contribute to the tailwinds.

Both the STAR Model and the beach metaphor invite dialogue about the complexity of change. You don't have to change the beach alone! Invite others into the work with you and see where the currents take you together. As Edgar and Peter Schein put it, "Culture is not a function, a result, a lever, an outcome, a tool. Culture is the multifaceted learned structure and practice of the people who lead and people who follow, people who work together and build a history that shapes the future."[11]

A STEM METAPHOR TO DRIVE THE POINT HOME: QUANTUM ENTANGLEMENT

Quantum entanglement is observed at the quantum scale where two or more particles can be intimately linked to each other even if separated. Any change performed on one of the particles affects the other, regardless of the distance between them. Organizational culture can be just as powerful as quantum entanglement. Core beliefs and ways of working can be so strong that even when you visit people around the globe, they behave similarly. That is when you know you have established a strong culture. On the other hand, if you imagine a company built through mergers and acquisitions that has not done a lot of work to integrate the new firms culturally, you might find that the company lacks a dominant culture and that individual units lack strong connections to the larger organization.

A STORY IN ACTION

After six grueling interviews, the organization finally extended an offer to Russel. Thrilled by getting through the process, he accepted the offer. As a department director, he was determined to put his spin on the hiring process to make it more streamlined and people friendly. At the end of his onboarding process, which took much longer than he felt necessary, he started developing his business strategy.

To best align his strategy with the organization's overall strategy, he started internally researching the organization's history. He noticed some cultural trends that explained why processes took so long to complete. The founders valued "perfection over production," believed that "slow and steady wins the race," and assumed that "if you have a great product, customers will come to you." While these are all great concepts in and of themselves, they undermined the firm's competitiveness in a marketplace that demanded fast and expedited services. His discovery helped explain why some antiquated processes were still used—it was because that's the way they have always been done.

Russel understood how challenging it can be to change organizational culture, so he started working on the five points of the STAR Model for his teams. The change he made to the hiring process centered on streamlining in a way that was still in alignment with the values of perfectionism and high quality but reduced the stall tactics and increased the capacity in the people element. He looked to reward slow and steady behavior—but not behavior that stopped necessary processes. By knowing and using the hidden forces of the culture, he fostered a microclimate within his team that helped change the broader culture into a future-focused organization.

REFLECTION QUESTIONS

- What are the values, beliefs, and assumptions of your company founders?
- Which of them are still in place, and which ones have shifted?
- How does the hidden culture of your organization impact the climate you are trying to create?
- Try out the STAR Model and consider what you might shift to reach the goals you would like to achieve.

FURTHER READING AND REFERENCES

On the more casual side . . . a resource to check out:

Galbraith, Jay R. (2022). *The Star Model.* https://www.jaygalbraith.com/images/pdfs/StarModel.pdf.

On the more academic side . . . references we used:

Clifton Jim, and Jim Harter. (2019). *It's the Manager: Moving from Boss to Coach*.

Schein, Edgar and Peter Schein (2019). *The Corporate Culture Survival Guide*.

5.3
MOTIVATING AND ENGAGING PEOPLE | INTRINSIC AND EXTRINSIC REWARDS

The ultimate freedom for creative groups is the freedom to experiment with new ideas. Some skeptics insist that innovation is expensive. In the long run, innovation is cheap. Mediocrity is expensive—and autonomy can be the antidote.

—**TOM KELLEY**, as quoted in Daniel Pink's *Drive*

THE PROBLEM These are just *some* of the challenges you might encounter that using both intrinsic and extrinsic rewards helps solve.	• Do you feel like your team is just showing up? • Do you struggle to get your team contributing to their fullest? • Do you want to know why your team members enjoy their work?

Now that you have stepped back and developed a strategy that aligns with your organization's culture, you're probably wondering how you get your people to execute your wonderful plan. This challenge is answered by understanding how to motivate and engage people. Given all the emotions and reactions we discussed in part 1, it's probably not a stretch of the imagination to consider that motivation varies from person to person and even within the one individual at different times. For example, you personally might have experienced more motivation at the beginning of a project and less motivation during the process. Knowing this, it can take even more effort to motivate others when you might not be feeling highly motivated or productive yourself.

Over the years, many leaders have been taught that people are motivated by rewards—traditionally, what we call extrinsic rewards. This influenced managers to think that people dislike work and only work for a paycheck. Therefore, to meet organizational goals, a manager needs to stay on top of his or her employees to prevent them from just collecting a paycheck while avoiding their work responsibilities. More modern approaches have emerged, however. Now managers are encouraged to view people as not just cogs on a wheel and to understand that, when people are given the opportunity, they are motivated to create solutions on their own just for the intrinsic rewards, such as personal learning and growth, satisfaction, self-esteem, etc.

So, which one is it—the paycheck or the hidden rewards? It turns out, it's both! In this topic, we share how you can use both extrinsic and intrinsic rewards to motivate your team and further engage them to deliver high performance.

MOTIVATING AND ENGAGING THROUGH INTRINSIC AND EXTRINSIC REWARDS

We can motivate others inwardly (intrinsic rewards) by addressing the things that are important to them and outwardly (extrinsic rewards) based on external outcomes they receive. But we need to be careful because matching the wrong reward to a person's motivation preference can actually reduce interest and result in low or no motivation. Further complicating the issue is that motivation directs, energizes, and sustains behavior across time and changing circumstances. Therefore, motivating employees is a dynamic process, not a process that occurs at a single point in time. As a manager or leader, you need to have a collection of tools in your tool belt to engage and motivate your employees, rather than a one-and-done, one-size-fits-all method. Consider the following examples of motivational factors:[12]

- **INTRINSIC FACTORS:** Having the opportunity for advancement, feeling one's job is aligned with one's internal purpose, having opportunities for learning, growth, fun, a sense of meaning or passion, and a personal sense of achievement.

- **EXTRINSIC FACTORS:** Pay, perks, bonuses and raises, work-life policies, other benefits, rewards, and recognition.

Whether you are motivating someone or not influences their job satisfaction. Job satisfaction refers to the general sense of contentment an employee has with their job. When an employee is dissatisfied, the source of their dissatisfaction tends to involve extrinsic factors, such as supervision, pay, company culture, and working conditions. In fact, these factors, according to Herzberg's Motivation Theory, are called *hygiene factors* because that is the extent of their impact—they maintain satisfaction.[13] However, it's important to know that just altering the dissatisfaction factors doesn't necessarily lead to satisfaction. As Daniel Pink states in his book *Drive*, "The problem with making an extrinsic reward the only destination that matters is that some people will choose the quickest route there, even if it means taking the low road. [But] when the reward is the activity itself—deepening learning, delighting customers, doing one's best—there are no shortcuts."[14]

That's why getting to satisfaction often involves expanding and tapping into intrinsic motivators. And, by tapping into intrinsic motivational factors, we also have the opportunity to lead to higher engagement. Engagement is different than satisfaction. While satisfied employees are content to stay, engaged employees are committed to their work and the overall company's success. Leaders have to engage the whole person at the individual level and invest in their cognitive, emotional, and physical energies to support their invisible intrinsic motivation process. By engaging the whole person, we engage individuals based on their identity and current life circumstances/stages. And we acknowledge that each individual may have completely different motivators than the next person. Three principles of engagement include the following:[15]

- **PSYCHOLOGICAL MEANINGFULNESS (COGNITIVE):** To feel worthwhile, useful, and valuable as a team member.

- **PSYCHOLOGICAL SAFETY (EMOTIONAL):** To feel able to express your full self without fear of negative consequences to your credibility or career.

- **PSYCHOLOGICAL AVAILABILITY (PHYSICAL):** To believe that one has all the resources required to invest oneself in the performance of a role

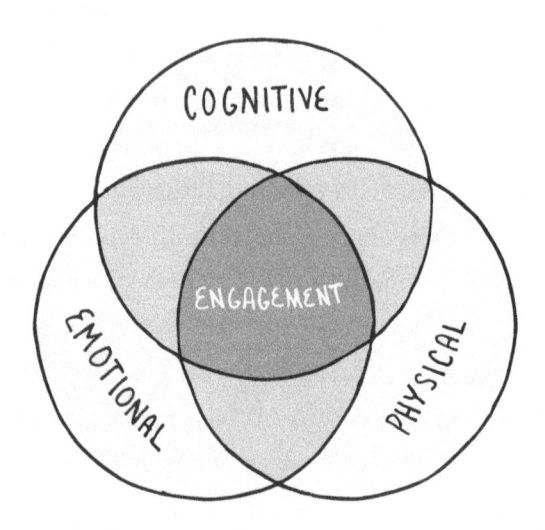

Notice how these three principles all tie back to intrinsic motivational factors. By leveraging adaptive leadership, we can see the various obstacles that lead to people being less engaged and less satisfied with their work and explain why they lack the motivation to do the work.

PUTTING THE CONCEPT INTO PRACTICE

How can you help employees feel a greater sense of meaningfulness, safety, and availability and get to engagement? Remember the acronym MAP, which is detailed in Daniel Pink's book *Drive*. Create a place and space for yourself and your teams to exercise mastery, autonomy, and purpose.

Mastery is the belief that one has the capability to learn and perform the different skills necessary to be successful and achieve one's goal.

- Give your employees time and opportunity to grow and develop.

- Give your employees a variety of projects or tasks that use and stretch their skills, but not at a pace that causes anxiety.

Autonomy is the need to feel in control and take direct actions to make a difference.

- Co-create work plans whenever possible and ask employees about their short-term and long-term career interests, and proactively include them in planning.

- Give people options and choices in what they do and how they do it.

- Watch out for micromanaging—focus on the outcomes you want and communicate those outcomes, rather than dictating how they get done (unless necessary for regulatory or other business-critical reasons).

Purpose speaks to an individual's need to feel unique while still experiencing a sense of belonging and connection with others.

- Give people space to have their own culture and identity, practices, priorities, and lifestyles. For example, don't assume that how you spent your weekend will be the same or similar to others. Be curious and develop connections to people as individuals.

- Introduce and connect team members to one another.

These are just a few ideas. What else would you add?

A STEM METAPHOR TO DRIVE THE POINT HOME: ANTIFRAGILITY

Antifragility is a property of systems that increases their ability to thrive after they experience stressors, shocks, volatility, noise, mistakes, faults, attacks, or failures. Instead of just dealing with the situation, the system uses the experience to improve. Supporting your employees through intrinsic motivational factors increases their antifragility, or engagement.

A STORY IN ACTION

Rajesh and the team have been working on a project for several months. At the project's onset, team members were all excited because they received lots of attention and resources. As time went on and new projects were added, the project seemed to become old news. The team members started to feel like they were underappreciated for all the behind-the-scenes hours they spent.

At the team meeting, Rajesh was picking up on the team's attitude about the project. The team meetings were normally a safe place to share ideas, but that hadn't been the case recently. The team members were throwing polite jabs at one another about the speed or quality of the work. The comebacks were things like: "Well, we've got this lack of resources now," "Why put all this effort into this project?" and "We're the only ones keeping this project alive."

Instead of Rajesh imposing his thoughts on the others about what was happening in the meeting, he asked the team, "What do we need to do to finish this project as strongly as we started?"

The team members opened up, and some named specific resources or listed vital parts of the process that had become an obstacle. Others said they needed more appreciation. "Sometimes we are treated like machines that are responsible for consistent output" was the sentiment shared. Some of the intermediate steps of the project were extremely detailed, and the team members felt that several of the nontechnical folks in the organization didn't understand this.

As the team members shared their thoughts and feelings, Rajesh noted the concerns. He went to his peers and supervisor to address their concerns. He found that several of his peers were experiencing this with their teams as well. As they brainstormed ways to engage and motivate their supervisees, they used their experiences to elevate their teams' satisfaction and performance.

REFLECTION QUESTIONS

- What helps you stay motivated?
- What intrinsic and extrinsic motivators do you already know help your team members contribute?
- What are ways you can motivate your team?
- How can you use intrinsic and extrinsic factors to help motivate them?

FURTHER READING AND REFERENCES

On the more casual side . . . a book to check out:

Pink, Daniel H. (2009). *Drive: The Surprising Truth About What Motivates Us.*

On the more academic side . . . references we used:

Deci, E. L., R. Koestner, and R. M. Ryan. (1998). "Extrinsic Rewards and Intrinsic Motivation: Clear and Reliable Effects." Unpublished manuscript, University of Rochester.

British Library. (2002). "Frederick Herzberg." https://www.bl.uk/people/frederick-herzberg.

Kahn, William A. (1990). "Psychological Conditions of Personal Engagement and Disengagement at Work." *Academy of Management Journal.* https://doi.org/10.2307/256287.

5.4

NAVIGATING INTERNAL POLITICS | DEFENSIVE ROUTINES AND COLLABORATIVE ADVANTAGE

Political awareness is simply an understanding of these power and influence webs and an ability to navigate them to achieve goals and get things done.

—DAVID OWASI

THE PROBLEM	• Do you feel like you are constantly justifying the business case for your team's needs?
These are just *some* of the challenges you might encounter that focusing on collaborative advantage helps solve.	• Do you feel like the competition in your workplace undermines productivity?
	• Do you often feel like you're caught in a power struggle?
	• Do you feel drained by the need to navigate internal politics to get work done?

Leaders in organizations are under tremendous pressure for all of their teams and departments to be highly coordinated and integrated to achieve the organization's mission. Depending on the organization, coordinating and integrating those efforts can vary wildly among teams and departments. This variety creates unique power dynamics, sometimes forcing internal competition, sometimes collaboration, sometimes independence, and sometimes codependence. Colloquially, these dynamics are talked about as navigating organizational politics.

The dynamics are often quite challenging to navigate since some of the power dynamics are not clearly understood. Sometimes, the organizational culture has created a competing versus collaborating attitude because of a scarcity mentality towards resources and perceived priorities. Other times, the "what's in it for me" attitude squashes the potential for collaborating to achieve the organization's mission.

As a leader or manager of a team, department, or larger unit of the organization, you are often the bridge between the individuals you lead and the rest of the organization. You are often at the center of asking for resources, ensuring projects are supported, and bringing information back to your team. Remember, you are not only responsible for your own success; you are also responsible for the success of the individuals in your team or department. In this topic, we will explore the concepts of collaboration, organizational defense routines, and what you can do to navigate them effectively as a leader.

NAVIGATING INTERNAL POLITICS BY UNDERSTANDING DEFENSIVE ROUTINES AND COLLABORATIVE ADVANTAGE

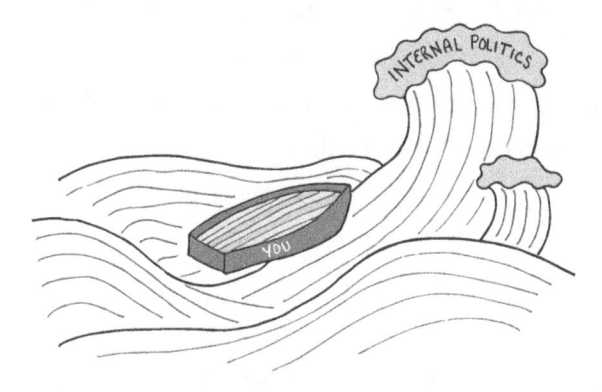

The ultimate goal of navigating power dynamics is to create effective collaboration across internal units, despite the tensions of competing for scarce resources. After all, you are all working for the same company and you all hope for success. One of the most common paradoxical tensions leaders face is the natural occurrence of both internal competition and collaboration. We know we can't meet organizational goals without one another, yet we compete for limited resources to maximize the potential of our own groups.

First, we will talk about the reasons why this occurs and the ways negative power dynamics manifest within organizations. Then, we will talk about collaboration. In the "Putting the Concept into Practice" section, we will share how you can err on the side of collaboration rather than competition.

Just like individuals display defensive behaviors when faced with the Four Fatal Fears, on a larger scale, organizations can also display defensive behaviors, called organizational defensive routines (ODR).[16] An ODR is any pattern of action that inhibits units of an organization from experiencing embarrassment or setbacks. These defensive routines can seem logical, which prevents identifying and solving the root cause of the embarrassment or setbacks. Though we often say we strive for high performance, most organizational systems would rather settle for mediocre performance rather than suffer occasional embarrassment or setbacks between moments of brilliance.

When engaging across the organization, the ODRs couldn't be clearer. These routines look like this:

- Competing for resources
- Calling for prioritization of one unit over others
- Selective or oppressive advancement
- Emphasis on a scarcity mentality
- Maneuvers that tell one unit's (more favorable) side of the story

On the topic of defensive routines, Chris Argyris says, "Whenever undiscussables exist, their existence is also undiscussable. Moreover, both are covered up, because rules that make important issues undiscussables violate espoused norms . . . It is very difficult to manage [organizational defense routines]. They continue to exist and proliferate because they are relegated to the realm of 'underground management' and all sides tacitly agree to this state of affairs. As a result, organizational defense routines often are very powerful."[17]

Interestingly, by partaking in these defensive routines, organizations actually invent activities that keep the very things they want to change from changing. In other words, by trying to look good or hoard resources as a unit, the trade-off is harmful to the broader organizational goals because the real challenges are suppressed.

A very common dysfunctional phenomenon that results from all of these defensive routines is termed *siloing*. A silo is when the functional responsibility of the team or department is more important than the organizational system in which it is embedded. Once teams and departments build those silos around themselves, the silos are very challenging to dismantle. That's not to say it is impossible. It just requires some special navigating and willingness to commit to collaboration as a partnership. It requires that all parties commit to taking care of one another for the greater good of the organization's success.

To overcome these challenges, we should seek to foster a culture of collaboration. How people perceive collaboration helps explain why internal competition exists. On the surface, most people refer to collaboration as "working together." But collaboration is much deeper than that. It gets at how willing people are to volunteer resources, share information, and establish mutual goals. Furthermore, it gets at a crucial power dynamic that is based on who has the status to make critical decisions and hold people accountable for outcomes and who doesn't have that power.

In the book *Managing to Collaborate*, Chris Huxham and Siv Vangen describe the distinction between collaborative advantage and collaborative inertia:

- **COLLABORATIVE ADVANTAGE:** The advantage you have because you are no longer limited by your own resources and expertise when you collaborate.

- **COLLABORATIVE INERTIA:** The frustration experienced by people who are collaborating when there is a lack of genuine positive outcomes.

Although their theory is geared towards collaboration between external organizations rather than within an organization, it's safe to say collaborative activities strive to move from inertia to advantage.

Just like we talked about with the Beach Model in the last topic, units express one of two organizational beliefs: espoused belief or enacted belief. Espoused beliefs are often easily regurgitated in conversations. They often limit individual and organizational learning because they reiterate static information in a dynamic environment. While a unit might say they have a collaborative belief, this could be an espoused belief—those that people report or describe. Enacted belief describes the values underlying what people actually do. When we explore the actual use of what the individual and organization need to meet their goals, we find lots of learning at the individual and system level. Your goals as a leader are to:

1. Act on your enacted beliefs, needs, and challenges to model a collaborative attitude with others in the organization.

2. Create safety and build relationships with other units to empower them to express their enacted beliefs, rather than sticking to the safety of espoused beliefs and defensive routines.

3. Influence up to champion collaboration over competition.

The organization's health depends on the balance of focus in the organization and the relationship to all its parts. What often gets missed is the understanding that collaboration within the organization is the competitive advantage against the competition. However, when we fail to collaborate internally, our ability to effectively address the competition outside the organization becomes compromised.

PUTTING THE CONCEPT INTO PRACTICE

The more collaboration needed between teams and departments, the greater the need to communicate. Communicating a message has both content (information) and relationship (how the communication is perceived).

To drive a collaborative environment, there first has to be some level of trust, so that communication is perceived from the beginning as having a positive intent. This trust is developed by listening deeply and by asking questions. By asking questions and actively listening to the answers, we can move the conversation towards collaboration and away from competition. We can move from collaborative inertia to collaborative advantage. Here are a few questions to begin with.

1. How comfortable are you with volunteering resources?
2. What level of information sharing are you comfortable with?
3. What mutual goals will benefit us both from our collaboration?
4. How can we have equal status in the decision-making?
5. What measure will we use to make sure we contribute equally and succeed as a result of our collaboration?

Some of the tips shared by Huxham and Vangen that are relevant for internal organization collaboration are:[18]

- Budget more time for collaborative activities than you expect to need.
- Be prepared to make trade-offs and compromises to your agenda, but be clear about your agenda.
- Build up mutual trust by setting and achieving small mutual wins.
- Don't assume your collaborators know your internal department's language, and don't be afraid to ask for clarification on their lingo.
- Have patience for power plays and keep a clear understanding of your strengths and weaknesses and sources of and threats to power. Seek to identify and understand the sources of and threats to your collaborators' power.

In part 4, we talked about the difference between having power over versus power to. This distinction can also be framed as the difference between generative and degenerative power, as shared by Adam Kahane in the book *Power and Love*. Kahane explores the need for complementarity between power and love tactics (feel free to replace with *care* or *empathy* if you resonate with a milder version of this language), rather than choosing one or the other. As Martin Luther King Jr. shares, "Power without love is reckless and abusive and love without power is sentimental and anemic."[19] Degenerative love seeks harmony and peace above all else, which creates a barrier to change. Degenerative power seeks to dominate others' will and point of view.

Power is not always assigned to those with financial control or hierarchical positional authority. Look out for more subtle ways power shows up, including the following:

- Who is the facilitator or leader for a meeting?
- Who chooses the location and timing of meetings?
- Who chooses who is involved in an activity?
- Who decides the name of an activity or project?
- Who tends to have the starting or the final word?
- Who tends to take up unequal time during a discussion?
- Who feels confident interrupting others?
- Who has direct access to key relationships or strategic partners?

Effective leaders seek to have both willfulness (power) and compassion (love) to determine future actions. By seeking to collaborate, great leaders harness the power of both/and thinking, rather than either/

or thinking, and capture the benefits of both generative power and generative love. When we don't walk together, we end up with power situations centered on oppression, scarcity, and authoritarian tactics that do not benefit the organization.

A STEM METAPHOR TO DRIVE THE POINT HOME: NETWORKS

A network comprises two or more connections that are linked in order to share resources. Starting with a single point of connection (called a node), the strength of a network increases as information freely flows back and forth between two nodes. As more nodes are introduced and connected, the network increases its size and structure. As the size and structure expand, the network requires more care in analyzing the current (free flow of information) and minimizing friction (obstacles to sharing information) to keep the network efficiently operating.

A STORY IN ACTION

Dawn took the management team that reports to her on an annual offsite retreat. She filled the agenda with team-building exercises designed to be fun and foster team communication, collaboration, and trust. She started with a fun icebreaker to get everyone's juices flowing and help them settle in as a team to start the day. Everyone was to share what they were most proud of (work or nonwork related) with the group. Dawn thought that everyone would have something different to share, and that this would be a good way to celebrate one another's accomplishments. But early in the day, it became obvious the managers were not excited to be there.

The first manager shared a proud work moment. But that anecdote bothered another manager because the first manager actually took resources from his department to achieve that success. Then another person shared their work success, which angered several managers because they felt she was just bragging. By the time everyone finished sharing, the room was thick with negative energy.

To help clear the air, Dawn called a fifteen-minute recess, so everyone could get some space. During that time, Dawn reflected on where she had experienced this in the past. It didn't take long for her to remember that she and her peers did the same thing at the senior manager's offsite. They left the retreat more siloed than when they arrived. She recognized that if she didn't do something different with this group, the same thing would happen.

When they came back, Dawn opened the conversation by pointing out what she had observed. She confessed that this was an organizational thing and that she and the management in that room had a choice. They could continue along the path they had started with. Or, they could begin to discuss the systems in their organization that fostered their silos and caused them to compete with one another and undercut one another's work, which resulted in more work, frustration, and aggravation. Dawn suggested they use the retreat to map out better ways to communicate and create a collaborative advantage.

REFLECTION QUESTIONS

- Are there things you and your teams are doing that undercut one another's work?

- What benefits are there to the competition that exists in the organization? Consequences?

- What organizational traps keep barriers to collaboration in circulation?

- How can those be replaced with conversations about what is really happening?

FURTHER READING AND REFERENCES

On the more casual side . . . books and resources to check out:

Argyris, Chris. (November 7, 2011). "Chris Argyris Talks About Culture and Management." https://youtu.be/le0yzpU5zHM.

Owasi, David. (August 24, 2020). "How to Navigate Office Politics and Build Influence." Medium. https://medium.com/swlh/how-to-navigate-office-politics-and-build-influence-4c575a567d2f.

On the more academic side . . . references we used:

Argyris, Chris. (1993). *Knowledge for Action: A Guide to Overcoming Barriers to Organizational Change*.

Huxham, Chris, and Siv Vangen. (2005). *Managing to Collaborate: The Theory and Practice of Collaborative Advantage*.

Kahane, Adam. (2009). *Power and Love: A Theory and Practice of Social Change*.

5.5

CULTIVATING COLLECTIVE WISDOM | LEARNING ORGANIZATIONS AND LEARNING 4.0 CAPABILITY

Imagine making the organization itself—and not separate, extra benefits—the incubator of capability.

— **KEGAN AND LAHEY,** *An Everyone Culture*

THE PROBLEM These are just *some* of the challenges you might encounter that developing a learning culture helps solve.	• Do you feel like your team is repeating patterns from the past? • Do you feel like other work is going on in the organization that overlaps with your team's work or might have relevant lessons for your team? • Do you feel like there are limited opportunities for you and your team members to develop your potential to the fullest?

At work, development is often an afterthought, and yet information is flowing at a rapid rate. So, to minimize cognitive overload, we have a tendency to treat everything as separate and divisible and, as we shared earlier, make mental shortcuts. For example, to understand how the organization functions, we analyze its structures and break them down into teams, departments, and functions. We evaluate our employees by breaking down what they do into skills, responsibilities, or job classifications. We diagram workflow and break it down into processes and procedures. We have become so accustomed to breaking things down into parts and pieces in order to digest the influx of information that we sometimes forget to look for what brings us together.

This bringing or binding together of all the parts and pieces is called *collective wisdom*. It is a perspective that invites relationships to form and deepens our regard for the underlying importance of connectedness. Connectedness is especially vital when dealing with massive complexity, which is today's most inevitable challenge in our large-scale organizations.

Most of us use collective wisdom in our personal lives. We have mentors or a collection of people we value for their insights. We look at multiple sources to learn what we don't know. But when it comes to organizations, we are less accustomed to leveraging the collective wisdom because of the insular hierarchies and job descriptions that break the collective wisdom into different parts and pieces. But today, in the digital age, we have better ways to efficiently collect wisdom on an organizational scale, and we have an even greater opportunity to foster collective wisdom and act on it. To make the most of these opportunities, we will explore the concept of the learning organization.

CULTIVATING COLLECTIVE WISDOM BY BUILDING A LEARNING ORGANIZATION

Sharing knowledge is not about giving people something or getting something from them. That is only valid for information sharing. Sharing knowledge occurs when people are genuinely interested in helping one another develop new capacities for action; it is about creating learning processes.

—PETER SENGE, *The Fifth Discipline*

For an organization to truly embrace collective wisdom, the organization's leaders need to commit to creating and being a learning organization.

A learning organization is an organization that is continually expanding its capacity to create its future. It enables agility, adaptability, and resilience—all of which help the organization to meet the growing demands of its industry. A learning organization unleashes employees and the business potential to create new lines of business that keep the organization on the cutting edge of the industry.

One thing to watch out for is that, in the attempt to be a learning organization, many leaders will create learning and development and organization development departments without empowering their people to have a learning mindset.

Setting up processes is one way to make things look like an organization values learning. But an organization needs to address both the learning organization structure and the employees' mindsets to truly be a learning organization. Employees must be open to continue acquiring new skills and capabilities, and the organization must reinforce habits of learning and feedback loops at every level of the organization.

To create habits at all levels, five core disciplines should be established. To create a learning organization, all five disciplines are necessary. Many of these disciplines are ones we have been building throughout the course of this book.

1. **SYSTEMS THINKING:** A shift from seeing parts to seeing the interconnectedness that gives a system its unique character.

2. **PERSONAL MASTERY:** Approaching life through a creative viewpoint.

3. **MENTAL MODELS:** Our theories of use (see topic 2.1) that determine how we make sense of the world and influence our actions.

4. **BUILDING A SHARED VISION:** Provides focus and energy to learn.

5. **TEAM LEARNING:** Happens when the alignment of the team members empowers them to function as a whole.

A Learning 4.0 mindset is a more tactical theory and model for building a learning mindset, developed by Patricia McLagan and published in her book *Unstoppable You*. A person with a Learning 4.0 mindset is someone who has the knowledge and skills to manage their own learning process, creating, in essence, a super learner. The Learning 4.0 model is based on the latest neuroscience and considers the challenges of learning in a digital age. Here are the seven steps learners can use to manage their own learning process:

1. **HEARING THE CALL:** Notice there is a learning opportunity.

2. **CREATING FUTURE PULL:** Put themselves into the future they want.

3. **SEARCH:** Find and use resources that can help them achieve their goals.

4. **CONNECTING THE DOTS:** Put the plan together and notice they are learning something.

5. **MINING FOR GOLD:** Process new information, deal with bias, and use techniques for efficiency and effectiveness.

6. **LEARNING TO LAST:** Turn information into something permanent within them.

7. **TRANSFER TO LIFE:** Transfer learning into the real world.

In the "Putting the Concept into Practice" section, we share how you, as a leader, can facilitate building employee capabilities using the Learning 4.0 mindset.

When we become managers and leaders, we rarely think our jobs will include much more than managing the work. But effective leaders find that managing timelines, deliverables, and resources are the tactical tasks that should be made as automated and efficient as possible. Effective leaders put more energy and a greater portion of their time on strategic tasks, such as seeing the big picture, understanding and removing cultural barriers to progress, motivating and engaging employees, and facilitating collective learning.

PUTTING THE CONCEPT INTO PRACTICE

As a leader, you are an important role model who can foster a learning culture. To create learning organizations, we need to value, create, and support learning. Here are some ways you can help.

- **VALUE LEARNING:** As we've shared throughout this book, actions grounded in beliefs are the most powerful demonstrations of values. What are your beliefs around the importance of learning? What might you need to change to be an effective team leader? Knowing that learning is an essential part of the organizational culture and team climates, make sure to:

    - Offer time and space to learn.

    - Know what your training department offers and how it ties into the capabilities your team most needs.

    - Budget time and funding for all employees to receive relevant training.

- Create a safe environment to learn and try, and learn and try again.
- Model learning yourself.

- **SUPPORT LEARNING:**

  - Make learning fun and easier to fit into the workday.
  - Have relevant material that lets the employee improve their skills in the moment they need to do so.
  - Support mentoring programs and informal opportunities to learn from others.
  - Ask what your training department does to support learning outside of the classroom and during the flow of work.
  - Make sure employees are aware of all the ways, times, and places they can learn.
  - Invest in or encourage platforms that promote learning—there are lots of technologies today that help social learning or learning in the moment; ask your training department what they are doing that's new in this area.
  - Help people develop the mindsets and capabilities they need for learning in this changing world of work.

- **CREATE LEARNING:**

  - Notice learning opportunities that occur and coach your employees.
  - Create feedback loops that happen in the moment and are unambiguous.

- Create habits to reinforce and celebrate learning—consider a culture of retrospectives, or specific points in time where the organization reflects together on what's been learned.

- Openly share lessons learned—successes and setbacks.

- If you are creating a learning experience for your team, be sure members have a learning agenda as well as a performance agenda. Don't start from intuition or scratch. Take time to improve your own skills using models like Patricia McLagan's Learning 4.0 model[20] or the Learning Cluster Design model,[21] so you can create an effective experience.

- Talk as a team about what's being learned—seek to connect the dots and mine for gold as per the Learning 4.0 model.

A STEM METAPHOR TO DRIVE THE POINT HOME: MACHINE LEARNING

Machine learning is a field of artificial intelligence that allows computers to learn without being explicitly programmed to learn a specific thing. Machine learning programmers are using various approaches to give computers the capability to learn. Machine learning relies first and foremost on the input data. Then, rather than being preprogrammed to take any action, a decision is expressed based on the data. Similarly, we don't want to get into a static, reactive mode based on limited pieces of data. We want to create a culture of taking in and sharing data, looking for patterns in the whole, and then moving forward together.

A STORY IN ACTION

Leo, the newly appointed VP, considered the annual strategic plan he was mostly responsible for implementing. He had spent time thinking about the different teams and their current strengths. In the past year, they had experienced successes in their launches of new products. As he thought about key lessons learned, he realized the team had gained a lot of wisdom related to communication and problem-solving in the moment.

This year, the plan called for moving back into a development phase. Leo thought some of the recent communication and problem-solving capabilities might still be helpful. But he wondered what else the teams might need. The industry had advanced a lot since the last time they started to develop a new product. Perhaps their team leaders needed to participate in some external conferences and then show and tell at department meetings. He also wondered whether any training refreshers his teams might need would be available through the training department.

He also wanted to hear what his teams thought. He put together a plan for holding a department retrospective. First, he'd use their online social community channel to ask the question "What are some skills you honed through last year's work?" That way, he could hear from as many people as possible. Then, at the live event, he'd get some help putting together themes and hearing what people are excited about as they think about the upcoming year.

Lastly, he thought about his own capabilities. He had created a great strategy, but what did he want to learn to make sure he could lead his team through a development phase rather than the urgent rush of the launch phase? One thing that came to mind was success metrics. How would he know whether his teams were on track or not? Leo could brush up on ROI metrics and team effectiveness metrics to help set his team up for success.

REFLECTION QUESTIONS

- Which of the five disciplines do you (and your organization) excel at?

- How can you (and your organization) incorporate the five disciplines?

- How ready is your organization to become a learning organization?

- What are your beliefs around time and effort spent on learning and the value of learning?

- Why do you think gathering the wisdom of your organization could be valuable?

- How can you empower learning to happen? How might you get in the way of learning?

- How can you help everyone in your organization own and develop the learning competence they will need to thrive?

FURTHER READING AND REFERENCES

On the more casual side . . . a book to check out:

McLagan, Patricia A. (2017). *Unstoppable You: Adopt the New Learning 4.0 Mindset and Change Your Life.*

On the more academic side . . . references we used:

Kadakia, Crystal, and Lisa Owens, M.D. (2020). *Designing for Modern Learning: Beyond ADDIE and SAM.*

Kegan, Robert, and Lisa Laskow Lahey. (2016). *An Everyone Culture: Becoming a Deliberately Developmental Organization.*

Senge, Peter M. (2010). *The Fifth Discipline: The Art and Practice of the Learning Organization.*

ACKNOWLEDGMENTS

To make this guide relevant to STEM professionals of all disciplines, we interviewed and consulted with Jeremy Hook, David Segal, Kathryn Mattox, Morgan Hook, Agata Kizerwetter, Thiago Avila, Peter Renner, and Walker White, tremendous professionals and dear friends in the field. We also appreciate contributor Patricia McLagan and reviewers Hortense Gerardo, Thomas Chan, Lynne Richards, and Drew Nizialek, who took time to review initial drafts and support the work. Towards the later stages of book development, we appreciated feedback from JaRae Birkeland, Lynne Richard, Jennifer Kahnweiler, Jessica Mohammad, and Lisa M. D. Owens. We are especially grateful to those who reviewed and provided their endorsements: Dr. Marshall Goldsmith, Darlene Christopher, Austin Lin, Ray Kung, Patrick Murphy, and Dr. Margaret Wheatley. We'd also like to thank our publishing team, editors Heather Stettler and Jessica Easto, design team led by Jared Dorsey, production manager Brian Welch, and everyone at Greenleaf who supported this book to become the best it can be.

NOTES

PART 1

1. Gary Wolf, "Steve Jobs: The Next Insanely Great Thing," interview with Steve Jobs, *Wired*, February 1, 1996, https://www.wired.com/1996/02/jobs-2.
2. Margaret Wheatley, *Perseverance* (Berrett-Koehler Publishers, 2010), 39.
3. Joseph Luft, "The Johari Window: A Graphic Model of Awareness in Interpersonal Relations," *Readings for the Human Interaction Library*, 79–83.
4. The Cynefin Model, developed by Dave Snowden.
5. Larry Wilson and Hersch Wilson, *Play to Win: Choosing Growth Over Fear in Work and Life*, first edition (Bard Press, 2004).
6. Henry Ford, https://www.motortrend.com/news/henry-fords-inspirational-quotes.
7. J. Tseng and J. Poppenk, "Brain meta-state transitions demarcate thoughts across task contexts exposing the mental noise of trait neuroticism," *Nature Communication* 11, no. 3480 (July 2020), https://doi.org/10.1038/s41467-020-17255-9.
8. J. Kabat-Zinn, *Mindfulness Meditation for Everyday Life* (Hyperion, 1994).
9. Wendy Tan, *Wholeness in a Disruptive World: Pearls of Wisdom from East and West* (Marshall Cavendish International [Asia], 2017), 137.
10. Rich Rosier, "A Conversation with David Rock on Self Regulation and Leadership," Linkage Inc., November 24, 2011, https://www.linkageinc.com/leadership-insights/a-conversation-with-david-rock-on-self-regulation-and-leadership.
11. Ryan Holiday, *Stillness Is the Key* (Portfolio, 2019), xv–xvi.
12. https://www.mindmapping.com.

13. C. Argyris, *Reasoning, Learning and Action: Individual and Organizational* (Jossey-Bass, 1982).
14. Jane Magruder Watkins, Bernard Mohr, and Ralph Kelly, *Appreciative Inquiry: Change at the Speed of Imagination*, second edition (Pfeiffer Press, 2011), 16.
15. Karn Bulsuk, "An Introduction to 5-why," 2009, https://www.bulsuk.com/2009/03/5-why-finding-root-causes.html.
16. H. A. Simon, "Decision-Making: Rational, Nonrational, and Irrational," *Educational Administration Quarterly* 29, no. 3 (1993): 392–411, https://doi.org/10.1177/0013161x93029003009.
17. J. S. Nairne, *Psychology of The Adaptive Mind*, third edition (Thomson Wadsworth, 2003).
18. Daniel Kahneman, *Thinking, Fast and Slow*, first edition (Farrar, Straus and Giroux, 2013), 35.

PART 2

1. Patricia Shaw, *Changing Conversations in Organizations: A Complexity Approach to Change* (Routledge, 2002), 10.
2. Shaw, *Changing Conversations*, 51.
3. Edgar H. Schein, *Humble Inquiry: The Gentle Art of Asking Instead of Telling* (Berrett-Koehler, 2013). Schein also talks about a fourth category, the "-1" dominant relationship, which we do not cover here.
4. Chris Argyris and Donald A. Schön, *Organizational Learning: A Theory of Action Perspective* (Addison Wesley, 1978); see also Peter M. Senge, Art Kleiner, Charlotte Roberts, and Bryan J. Smith, *The Fifth Discipline Fieldbook* (Currency, Doubleday, 1994).
5. K. Patterson, J. Grenny, R. McMillan, and A. Switzler, *Crucial Conversations: Tools for Talking When Stakes Are High* (McGraw-Hill, 2012), 22.
6. Samuel J. Ling, William Moebs, and Jeff Sanny, *University Physics, Volume 2*, https://commons.erau.edu/oer-textbook/2.

7. David Rock, *Your Brain at Work* (Harper Business, 2020), 105.
8. Don Miguel Ruiz, *The Four Agreements: A Practical Guide to Personal Freedom* (Amber–Allen Publishing, 2018).
9. Adam Grant, *Give and Take: A Revolutionary Approach to Success* (Viking, 2013), 10.
10. Grant, *Give and Take*, 258.
11. L. G. Scanlon and A. Vernick, *Five Minutes: (That's a Lot of Time) (No, It's Not) (Yes, It Is)* (G. P. Putnam's Sons, 2019).

PART 3

1. https://developers.google.com/style/inclusive-documentation.
2. B. W. Tuckman, "Developmental Sequence in Small Groups," *Psychological Bulletin* 65, no. 6 (1965): 384–399.
3. Connie Gersick, "Time and Transition in Work Teams: Toward a New Model of Group Development," *Academy of Management Journal* 31, no. 1 (1988), https://doi.org/10.2307/256496.
4. Gersick, "Time and Transition."
5. Kenwyn K. Smith and David N. Berg, *Paradoxes of Group Life: Understanding Conflict, Paralysis, and Movement in Group Dynamics* (Wiley & Sons, 1997), 14.
6. Jean Vanier, *Becoming Human* (Paulist Press, 2008), 18.
7. Fleming Ray, "General Systems Theory: A Knowledge Domain in Engineering Systems," ESD.83 Research Seminar in Engineering Systems, October 25, 2000, https://studylib.net/doc/18760994/general-systems-theory--a-knowledge-domain-in, 2.
8. Richard Fagerlin, *Trustology: The Art and Science of Leading High-Trust Teams* (Wise Guys Publishing, LLC, 2013), 10.
9. Smith and Berg, *Paradoxes*, 120.
10. Stephen M. R. Covey, *The Speed of Trust: The One Thing That Changes Everything* (Free Press, 2006), 6.

11. W. A. Kahn, "Psychological Conditions of Personal Engagement and Disengagement at Work," *Academy of Management Journal* 33, no. 4 (December 1990): 708, https://doi.org/10.2307/256287.

12. Doug Crandall and Matt Kincaid, *Permission to Speak Freely: How the Best Leaders Cultivate a Culture of Candor* (Berrett-Koehler, ReadHowYouWant large print edition, 2017), 13.

13. K. A. Jehn and C. Bendersky, "Intragroup Conflict in Organizations: A Contingency Perspective on the Conflict-Outcome Relationship," *Research in Organizational Behavior* 25, no. 1 (2003): 187–242, https://doi.org/10.1016/S0191-3085(03)25005-X.

14. Kerry Patterson, Joseph Grenny, Ron McMillan, and Al Switzler, *Crucial Conversations: Tools for Talking When Stakes Are High* (McGraw-Hill, 2012).

15. Patterson et al., *Crucial Conversations*, 9.

16. Patterson et al., *Crucial Conversations*, 20.

17. Patterson et al., *Crucial Conversations*, 34.

18. W. Gibb Dyer, Jr., Jeffrey H. Dyer, and William G. Dyer, *Team Building: Proven Strategies for Improving Team Performance*, fifth edition (Jossey-Bass, 2013), 4.

19. B. Johnson, *Polarity Management: Identifying and Managing Unsolvable Problems* (HRD Press, Inc., 1996).

20. Dyer et al., *Team Building*, 134.

21. T. Rath, *StrengthsFinder 2.0* (Gallup Press, 2007).

22. Tilt 365, "Strengths Assessment: You Are So Much More Than Your Personality," 2022, https://www.tilt365.com.

PART 4

1. Editorial Board, "COVID Has Shown the Power of Science–Industry Collaboration," *Nature* 594, no. 302 (2021), https://doi.org/10.1038/d41586-021-01580-0.

2. Warren G. Bennis, *On Becoming a Leader* (Basic Books, 1989).
3. Peter Drucker, *The Effective Executive* (HarperCollins Publishing, 2006).
4. Ronald A. Heifetz, Marty Linsky, and Alexander Grashow, *The Practice of Adaptive Leadership: Tools and Tactics for Changing Your Organization and the World* (Harvard Business Press, 2009).
5. Heifetz et al., *The Practice of Adaptive Leadership*, 7.
6. Allan Mørch, "[Infographic] A One Hour Meeting Is Never Just a One Hour Meeting," AskCody, August 31, 2017, https://www.askcody.com/blog/infographic-a-one-hour-meeting-is-never-just-a-one-hour-meeting.
7. Rollo May, as quoted in Adam Kahane, *Power and Love: A Theory and Practice of Social Change* (Berrett-Koehler Publishers, 2009), 7.
8. Kahane, *Power and Love*.
9. Kahane, *Power and Love*, 17.
10. Kahane, *Power and Love*.
11. Amy Edmonston, "Psychological Safety," *Disrupt Yourself Podcast*, episode 115, June 18, 2019, https://whitneyjohnson.com/amy-edmondson.
12. Kahane, *Power and Love*, 17.
13. Jim Clifton and Jim Harter, *It's the Manager: Moving from Boss to Coach* (Gallup Press, 2019).
14. https://dictionary.apa.org/groupthink.
15. Gibb W. Dyer, Jr., Jeffrey H. Dyer, and William G. Dyer, *Team Building: Proven Strategies for Improving Team Performance* (Jossey-Bass, 2013), 76.
16. H. M. Robert III, T. J. Honemann, T. J. Balch, D. E. Seabold, and S. Gerber, *Robert's Rules of Order*, twelfth edition (PublicAffairs, 2020).
17. History.com Editors, "Nikola Tesla," updated March 13, 2020, https://www.history.com/topics/inventions/nikola-tesla.

18. Erik Gregersen, "Tesla, Inc," Britannica, updated September 1, 2021, https://www.britannica.com/topic/Tesla-Motors.
19. InnerDrive, "Why the Middle Is the Hardest Part of a Task," 2022, https://blog.innerdrive.co.uk/middle-hardest-part-of-task.
20. Marshall Goldsmith, "Feedforward," http://www.marshallgoldsmithfeedforward.com/html/FeedForward-Tool.htm.
21. Michael de la Maza, "The Guide to Retrospectives—Remote or in Person," Miro, October 2020, https://miro.com/guides/retrospectives.

PART 5

1. J. T. Klein, "Sustainability and Collaboration: Cross-Disciplinary and Cross-Sector Horizons," *Sustainability* 12, no. 4 (2020), https://doi.org/10.3390/su12041515, 2.
2. Michael E. Porter, *Competitive Advantage* (The Free Press, 1985), 11–15.
3. "The Five Competitive Forces That Shape Strategy," *Harvard Business Review* interview with Michael E. Porter, June 30, 2008, https://www.youtube.com/watch?v=mYF2_FBCvXw.
4. Gareth Morgan, *Images of Organization* (Sage Publications, 2006).
5. Thomas G. Cummings and Christopher G. Worley, *Organization Development and Change* (Cengage, 2018).
6. Margaret J. Wheatley, *Leadership and the New Science: Discovering Order in a Chaotic World* (Berrett-Koehler, 2006).
7. Wheatley, *Leadership and the New Science*, 48.
8. Jim Clifton and Jim Harter, *It's the Manager: Moving from Boss to Coach* (Gallup Press, 2019).
9. Edgar Schein and Peter Schein, *The Corporate Culture Survival Guide*, third edition (Wiley & Sons, 2019), 4.
10. Jay R. Galbraith, *The Star Model*, accessed May 4, 2022, https://www.jaygalbraith.com/images/pdfs/StarModel.pdf.

11. Schein and Schein, *The Corporate Culture Survival Guide*, 4.
12. William A. Kahn, "Psychological Conditions of Personal Engagement and Disengagement at Work," *Academy of Management Journal* 33, no. 4 (1990): 692–724, https://doi.org/10.2307/256287.
13. "Frederick Herzberg," British Library, accessed May 4, 2022, https://www.bl.uk/people/frederick-herzberg.
14. Daniel H. Pink, *Drive: The Surprising Truth About What Motivates Us* (Riverhead Books, 2009), 51.
15. E. L. Deci, R. Koestner, and R. M. Ryan, "Extrinsic Rewards and Intrinsic Motivation: Clear and Reliable Effects," unpublished manuscript, University of Rochester, 1998.
16. Chris Argyris, *Knowledge for Action: A Guide to Overcoming Barriers to Organizational Change* (Jossey-Bass, 1993).
17. Chris Argyris, as quoted in Leni Wildflower and Diane Brennan, *The Handbook of Knowledge-Based Coaching* (Jossey-Bass, 2011), 438; originally from Chris Argyris, *On Organizational Learning* (Wiley-Blackwell, 1999), 159.
18. Chris Huxham and Siv Vangen, *Managing to Collaborate: The Theory and Practice of Collaborative Advantage* (Routledge, 2005).
19. Martin Luther King, Jr., "Power at Its Best Is LOVE," https://www.youtube.com/watch?v=SsvSq5_vbL4, at 0:29 sec.
20. Patricia A. McLagan, *Unstoppable You: Adopt the New Learning 4.0 Mindset and Change Your Life* (Association for Talent Development, 2017).
21. Learning Cluster Design Group, https://learningclusterdesign.com.

ABOUT THE AUTHORS

CRYSTAL KADAKIA is an organization development consultant, two-time TEDx speaker, and chemical engineer. Her career began as an engineer for Procter & Gamble, then transitioned to a role as a training manager. She left the corporate workplace to problem-solve cultural challenges through her own consultancy. Since then, she has spoken on international stages, written several books, including *The Millennial Myth* (Berrett-Koehler, 2018) and *Designing for Modern Learning* (Association for Talent Development, 2020), and she has consulted with a wide range of companies representing many industries. Currently, she operates two businesses. She is the CEO of the Learning Cluster Design Group, a firm changing the way learning occurs in organizations from in the classroom to in the flow of work. She also works independently as a consultant with executive leadership and project teams in nonprofit and for-good ventures on strategy formation and process design. Her goal is to apply her multifaceted experience and strengths to furthering the work of conservation and sustainability-oriented organizations.

Taylor Overton Photography

JANETTE WILLIAMS, IMBA, PhD, is an organizational psychologist and business consultant, researcher, and academic instructor. With more than thirty years of experience and extensive insight working in private, public, nonprofit, and government sectors, Janette uses a systems approach to integrate the wholeness of individuals, teams, and organizations to achieve optimal performance. Committed to staying intellectually curious, she uses her knowledge and expertise to challenge herself and others to reach their full potential.

She has three major goals in life: (1) to help as many people as possible reach their goals, (2) to have no gas left in her tank when she dies, and (3) to educate college students to become highly employable.

ABOUT THE ILLUSTRATOR

Lakin Nicole Photo

MICHELLE SMILEY, MBA, is a technology and business consultant with a love for artwork and creative expression. Her career began in engineering with an energy industry EPIC firm and progressed into both product and project management and sales and marketing. Michelle pursued a fifteen-year corporate career in engineering, management, and growth before leaving to pursue bespoke development, technology and business consulting, and other entrepreneurial endeavors. Michelle's goal is to foster continual learning and love of learning in others to help them reach new opportunities.